Toddler Parenting Success:

2 Books in 1: Toddler Discipline + Toddler Potty Training for Effective Toddler Care & Development

Toddler Discipline: Proven Toddler Discipline Strategies for Stress & Guilt-Free Parenting

Toddler Potty Training: Incredibly Simple 2-Day Potty Training that Works

Marie C. Foster

About this Bundle:

Congratulations on owning *Toddler Parenting Success: 2 Books in 1: Toddler Discipline + Toddler Potty Training for Effective Toddler Care & Development*, and thanks for doing so.

What you are about to read is a collection of two separate books on Toddler Care and Development that would benefit you as a parent. The first book will be about Toddler Discipline while the second book will discuss Toddler Potty Training.

Book 1:
Toddler Discipline: Proven Toddler Discipline Strategies for Stress & Guilt-Free Parenting

Here you will learn how to become a better toddler parent, by teaching you to raise your little one with proper discipline.

Book 2:
Toddler Potty Training: Incredibly Simple 2-Day Potty Training that Works

Here you will learn the best methods for potty training your toddler. Whether your toddler is a girl or boy, you should now be armed with the knowledge to make toilet training happen in just two days.

Thanks again for owning this book!

Let us begin with the first book in the Toddler Parenting Success bundle:

Toddler Discipline:

Proven Toddler Discipline Strategies for Stress & Guilt-Free Parenting

Marie C. Foster

© **Copyright 2018 by Marie C. Foster - All rights reserved.**

The contents of this book may not be reproduced, duplicated or transmitted without direct written permission from the author.

Under no circumstances will any legal responsibility or blame be held against the publisher for any reparation, damages, or monetary loss due to the information herein, either directly or indirectly.

Legal Notice:

This book is copyright protected. This is only for personal use. You cannot amend, distribute, sell, use, quote or paraphrase any part or the content within this book without the consent of the author.

Disclaimer Notice:

Please note the information contained within this document is for educational and entertainment purposes only. Every attempt has been made to provide accurate, up to date and reliable complete information. No warranties of any kind are expressed or implied. Readers acknowledge that the author is not engaging in the rendering of legal, financial, medical or professional advice. The content of this book has been derived from various sources. Please consult a licensed professional before attempting any techniques outlined in this book.

By reading this document, the reader agrees that under no circumstances are is the author responsible for any losses, direct or indirect, which are incurred as a result of the use of information contained within this document, including, but not limited to, —errors, omissions, or inaccuracies.

Table of Contents

Introduction

Chapter 1: Essentials of Effective Toddler Discipline

Chapter 2: Understanding Toddler Behavior

Chapter 3: Effective Communication: How to Connect with your Child

Chapter 4: Discipline Strategies

Chapter 5: Stressed Out? How to Remain Calm

Chapter 6: Common Mistakes and How to Avoid Them

Chapter 7: How to Discipline a Special Needs Child

BONUS Chapter: When Strategies don't seem to Work

Conclusion

Introduction:

One of the biggest struggles that parents face is knowing how to discipline their toddlers. If you have ever heard of the 'terrible twos', then you may have an inkling of how difficult it can be—for more reason than one.

During the toddler years, your baby starts to define their place in the world. They are going to challenge your authority, push boundaries, and throw fits when the world does not move according to how they think it should.

The second reason that the toddler years are so difficult is because of the barrage of information that parents must sort through. Your child's doctor, friends and other parents, your parents and in-laws, and all sorts of people will think that they know the best way to raise your child. Through all this input that they offer, you must decide what is valuable and what just doesn't fit within your parenting style.

The other problem comes when trying to find information on the Internet. Like in real life, information comes from various sources—and much of it is contradictory to other ideas you find.

Fortunately, by owning this book, you are taking the first step in finding some solid, accurate information about disciplining your toddler. The ideas in this book are written using a balance between scientific information and personal experience raising my boys, who are 2 and 4 currently.

With my first son, I had a lot of trial-and-error and, of course, the input of anyone that I talked to about my kids. I have created this book with a desire to educate parents about different discipline strategies that exist, so you don't have to dig for information and guess about what works and doesn't work. The strategies are proven effective, from my home to yours, and heavily based on scientific studies that have been done concerning toddler discipline. At the end of the book, there is also a chapter on disciplining special needs kids, which requires a slightly different technique than most toddlers.

This book is going to serve a great purpose in your life. It will help you develop discipline strategies that you can use without feeling guilty or stressed. It is not uncommon for parents to question their methods, especially if they feel they must yell or hit their child. The truth is, however, that you do not have to scream at your child or spank them to get their attention. By employing the strategies that follow in this book, you will learn how to properly discipline your child, so they grow into a well-rounded, emotionally healthy adult.

It is never too late to take the first step to proper toddler discipline. So, let's get started!

Chapter 1: Essentials to Effective Toddler Discipline

Chapter 1: Essentials to Effective Toddler Discipline

From the moment your child comes into the world, its eyes are on you. As he or she learns and grows, you will see yourself in the things that they do—like the way that your baby smiles or the chuckle they get when you tickle them. Unfortunately, as babies grow into toddlers, they become more defiant versions of themselves. They start to make their place in the world, test boundaries, and are prone to occasional fits of outrageous behavior, as they try to explore all that is around them. It's as your child leaves infancy and moves into these trying times that toddler discipline becomes necessary for healthy development of your little boy or girl.

One of the problems that parents sometimes face is finding a toddler discipline strategy that they can use without feeling guilty. For example, when you spank your child, it does not make you feel better following the punishment. For most parents, it makes them feel worse and question their abilities. Fortunately, by picking up this book, you have made the first commitment to stress-free and guilt-free parenting.

What is Toddler Discipline?

Toddler discipline has a profound effect on your child's future and mental health. While the word discipline can come across as harsh under certain contexts, this is caused by a misinterpretation of its meaning. Discipline should not always mean punishment. When it comes to toddler discipline, it means teaching and guidance, rather than punishing your toddler when they do not listen to you.

There will be times that you want to punish your toddler. This is because as your child learns from you, he or she is given the choice as to whether they listen or not. They will not always be obedient—and this warrants some kind of response. If you do not respond to their behaviors at all, they will continue to push boundaries and escalate.

Discipline Myths

There are many ways that you can discipline a toddler, however, not all methods are going to work. There are many myths regarding disciplining children, including:

- Yelling Louder Will Get My Toddler's Attention- It can be very easy to yell at a toddler, especially as they defiantly knock over their fourth drink that day or throw their toys through the house. The problem with yelling is that when it becomes normalized, it loses its effectiveness. Instead of hearing you because you are yelling louder, your child will learn to tune it out and go on with their bad behavior. This means when it is important, or they are doing something dangerous, you will not be able to get their attention.

- My Parents Spanked Me, and I Turned Out Okay- According to a study published in 2014, 65% of women and 76% of men supported spanking a misbehaving child. However, numerous studies have proven that spanking does little to achieve a toddler's behavior. Not only will it not change bad behavior in the long-term, it has shown positive correlations to antisocial tendencies, aggression, and poor mental health. Some studies even suggested that the long-term results of an occasional smack on the bottom had the same effect as child abuse.
- Negotiation Never Works- People who are concerned with being overly permissive and ending up

with a 'bad' kid will tell you that you should never negotiate with a child. However, that is simply not the truth. The key to negotiation is to let the child make a decision, but to keep the cards in your hand by giving them a few acceptable options and then letting them make a choice. We will explore this idea more in depth later in the book.

- You Should Never Say 'Yes'- Another common myth is that if you tell your child 'yes,' you are failing to give them the boundaries that they need to thrive. But, what if your toddler is asking for something reasonable? If you are worried about setting boundaries, follow the 'yes' with a condition. Then, explain the reason why before your toddler has a chance to ask. For example, "Yes, you can play with Play-Doh but only if you pick up your toys. Otherwise, we will not be able to see any Play-Doh that has fallen on the floor and needs picked up when you are done."

- Strict Parents Are Good Parents- It is hard not to judge when you see a toddler flailing on the floor of the supermarket, thinking that the parent needs to be stricter. The problem with this mindset is that when we are too strict with kids, we do not teach them empathy, compassion, and understanding. After all, they are looking to us as role models on how to treat other people.

- You Should Not Have to Repeat Yourself- The truth is that toddlers have a short attention span. While they will get the general message you are trying to send from day-to-day, you should expect to repeat yourself—a lot. Just like with learning counting, colors, shapes, and the alphabet, toddlers learn through repetition that helps form the connections in their mind. It can be frustrating when you feel like you are constantly repeating yourself, but it is necessary to communicate clearly with your toddler.

Do not worry if you have been guilty of any of these things in the past—it is never too late to take a new approach to discipline. In this book, you will learn many effective tactics for discipline, designed to give you a variety of methods for different situations you may encounter with your toddler. Through your own personal journey with toddler discipline, your parenting style, study, and research, you will be able to shape a disciplinary plan that works. Additionally, you will learn more about what you should expect from your toddler—including behavior and response to discipline.

As you read, keep in mind that raising any child (not just yours) comes with its challenges. They can cause stress, self-doubt, and worry over whether you are getting it right—but just take a deep breath. These days will be over before you know it and raising a child is always a rewarding experience in the end.

Why Toddler Discipline is Important

The key to toddler discipline is a balance. You cannot punish your child so much that they have psychological scars, which last long after childhood. However, you cannot be so permissive that your toddler does not learn boundaries. You must be strict, but you also must care enough that your toddler understands that the rules you set forth are for their best interest. Some of the benefits of good toddler discipline include:

- Prevents Physical Struggles- When you choose aggressive methods like spanking, it can cause the problem with your toddler to escalate. They also learn that this behavior is acceptable. By finding a better discipline problem, you can encourage your son or daughter to behave without physical violence.

- Better Management of Anxiety- When a toddler looks to you to set boundaries, they are testing you to reassure themselves. Your toddler does not want to be in charge. What they do want is to feel assured that you are in control of the situation. If a child does not have this, they can develop anxiety because they feel pressured to set adult boundaries and make adult situations.

- Proper Discipline Encourages Safety- The major goal of

discipline should never be to punish—it should be to ensure your child's safety and health. Consequences must be given so that your toddler knows they cannot run out into the street without looking. They can also be used to promote health and prevent obesity. For example, teaching your toddler to eat a wide range of healthy foods and saying 'no' to obsessive snacking habits.

- Better Management of Frustration, Anger, and Other Emotions- If you give in every time that your child has a temper tantrum, you are sending the message that he or she should continue to act this way to get what they want. When you discipline your child by ignoring mild tantrums, your toddler learns that society will not do what they want if they act in that manner. Time out also has a purpose following an angry outburst—by reinforcing the idea of taking time to reflect on the anger. Finally, using praise helps deal with frustration, especially when you credit your child with continuing to work hard at something, despite their frustration.

- Encourages Good Choices- When you discipline your toddler appropriately, you teach them how to make decisions. Healthy discipline can encourage them to consider alternative ways for getting needs met. Some of the skills that can be learned include self-regulation, impulse control, and problem solving. Rather than focusing on punishments, teach your child consequences. These are more effective in teaching them about their mistakes, making it less likely that they will choose poorly in the future.

Disciplining Your Toddler: What to Expect

Below, you will find some general tips for toddler discipline. Specific techniques will be discussed later in the book, but this is an overview of how you might apply these techniques to disciplining your child:

- Positive Reinforcement- Praise and positive reinforcement will go a long way in teaching your child to behave well. When you tell them they are doing something good, and your actions and tone of voice reflect this positivity, they will get good feelings from it. The positive way they are experiencing the activity will make it more likely they will repeat this good behavior in the future.

- Ignore the Bad (to an Extent)- When you child throws a temper tantrum, they are trying to get your attention. If you yell or respond, you are giving them what they want. Provided they are not harming themselves or someone else, let your toddler cry it out. This can be embarrassing if you are somewhere like the store, but if you give into what they want just to get them to be quiet, you are encouraging them to recreate the scenario in the future. If you cannot stand the temper tantrum, leave any groceries you have not paid for behind and walk out to the car. Let them sit inside with you until they can calm down or go home and try shopping another time.

- Logical Consequences- This form of discipline involves creating a consequence if your toddler behaves. For example, tell your child (do not yell) that if they do not pick up their toys, you will take them away for the day. Set a time limit or react if your child does not start moving to pick up the toys. Once they do not listen, follow through on the consequence immediately and ignore their protest/tantrum that may result.

- Natural Consequences- If your child is not doing something dangerous, one of the best things you can do is let the situation unfold naturally. The key is not coming to their rescue after the event, no matter how much they cry. For example, imagine that your toddler keeps throwing their cookies on the floor. Instead of yelling or punishing them, warn them that they will not have any cookies if they throw them all on the floor. Let this natural consequence unfold and do not give them any more cookies once they have run out.

- Redirection- When your child seems like they might make a fuss over what you have just told them not to do, re-direct them. For example, imagine that two siblings are fighting over a toy. You can give it to the child that had it first if you saw what happened. Otherwise, remove the toy and put it up. Redirect the siblings to a new activity, either one that they can do together or to two separate activities that they can work on alone.
- Time Out- It is not uncommon for parents to protest the time out method, especially if their child is resistant. The problem in these cases is not usually the technique (time out) but the way that time out is enforced. Before your child

has a chance to behave poorly, set rules with them about the types of behaviors (hitting, throwing toys, etc.) that will get them in time out. This should be limited to 2-3 things that your child should remember. Then, you will set a location and length of time for the time out. If the infraction happens, stick to the guidelines you set, regardless of your toddler's reaction. Another option is using one area for quiet time and another for time out, which is the more severe consequence. We will talk more deeply about this later.

- Withholding Privileges- When you withhold privileges, it must be done in a way that your toddler can form the connection between what is being taken away and the bad behavior. You can take away something valuable to your child, like a toy, television, or another privilege, but you should never take away something that is a necessity (like food). You should also do the punishment immediately since children under 6-7 years of age do not have the mental capacity to understand something like losing TV in the evening being connected to refusing to pick up their toys that morning.

CHAPTER SUMMARY:

1. Toddler discipline should not have the goal of punishing misbehavior, but teaching between right and wrong.

Toddlers are at a point in their life when they are very impressionable and the way that you choose to discipline them can affect them greatly later in life. There are many myths regarding discipline that you should take note of, including that yelling and spanking are effective. Do your research to learn about the scientific reasons that discipline may or may not work, rather than listening to the anecdotes of other people's advice.

2. Disciplining your toddler is about balance. You will need to set rules firmly, but you must also show compassion and understanding. When discipline is done correctly, toddlers grow into well-behaved, well-rounded children. Some of the benefits include prevention of physical altercations,

anxiety management, the safety of your toddler, emotional regulation, and encouragement of good choices.

3. There are many discipline strategies that will work in this book. What it boils down to is what is most effective for your child. Often, you will vary the discipline based on the bad behavior. Some of the techniques that will be discussed in this book include positive reinforcement, ignoring bad behavior, logical and natural consequences, redirecting, time out, and withholding things.

YOUR QUICK START ACTION STEP: EVALUATE DISCIPLINE MYTHS

Is there anything specific that you have

heard regarding toddler discipline that you are skeptical about? Take twenty or thirty minutes to learn what you can about the most common discipline myths and take stock of which ones you may use in your parenting style. Do not worry if you find a few—no parent is perfect. By identifying these, you can start to understand which aspects of your toddler discipline practices that you may want to alter or replace.

Chapter 2: Understanding Toddler Behavior

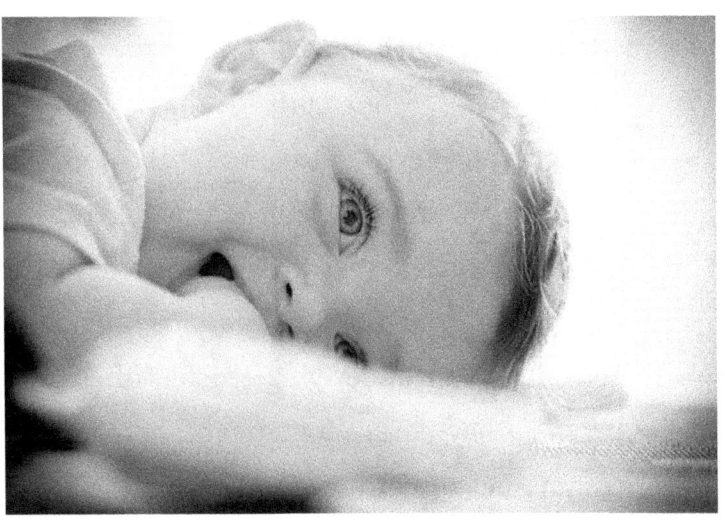

Chapter 2: Understanding Toddler Behavior

If you are like me, or almost any other parent for that matter, there are times when your child's behavior just has you asking 'why?' The truth is that even though you see your toddler's behavior as strange or frustrating, it is most likely a normal reaction to the changes they are going through in life. Toddlers often act out for an underlying reason, often because they do not understand how to communicate their needs and what they are going through.

Why Your Toddler Doesn't Listen

The 'Terrible Twos' are most likely to happen between the ages of 2 and 3. During this time, toddlers are learning that they are individuals apart from their parents or other caregivers. They strike out as independent entities, which leads to their desire to assert themselves during this stage. Toddlers are also more likely to act independently and want to try things for themselves, as well as communicate what they like and do not like. This is the reason that most toddlers choose not to listen to what we tell them—they are trying to express themselves and set themselves apart from their parents. Even so, this can be problematic when we are trying to provide guidance and keep them safe. There are several reasons that your child may be acting out, including:

- They Don't Understand Their Feelings- The toddler age is when your child is emotionally mature enough to start experience emotions. This includes complex feelings like embarrassment, pride, guilt, frustration, joy excitement, jealousy, anger, and shame. Another problem is how quickly their mood changes—one moment your child can happily be licking a popsicle and the next they may be sobbing because some of it melted onto their hand.
- They Lack Self-Control- Another reason toddlers may act out is because they do not know to express how they are feeling. This means that when they are angry with someone, for example, they do not know how to say, "I am

mad" or even relate what they are feeling with anger. Instead, they may lash out by throwing a tantrum, hitting, or screaming. As your child learns to identify these emotions and appropriately respond to them, they will start to make better behavioral choices.

- They are Over stimulated- Have you ever spent a day out in the sun and been exhausted at the end of it? This is from overstimulation from sunlight in your eyes and on your skin. Toddlers can experience sensory overload too, though they experience it with much less stimulation than adults. Sometimes, toddlers need time to themselves and to be away from it all. If you have ever had a long, exhausting day and then been short-tempered with your partner later, then you have experienced a similar feeling to this.

- They Have a Need that is Not Being Met- Toddlers are incredibly sensitive to all things during this time, not just their emotions. If your child is hungry, thirsty, or over-tired, chances are they are going to misbehave. Unfortunately, they cannot always identify these things and tell you what they need.
- They Want Attention- When toddlers are looking for their parents to pay attention, they will go to any lengths to get it. Have you ever told your toddler that you were in the middle of something, only to find them

getting in trouble not even five minutes later? Odds are, when you do not give them the attention they are seeking, they will misbehave to get negative attention instead. Either way, your focus is on them.

- They Are Having a Bad Day- One of the things that parents often forget is that they have bad days. Some days, you may feel 'off' or irritable for what seems like no reason. Toddlers can have this problem too. When we do not give them the same regard for their feelings that adults have, it does not empathy or compassion.

How Understanding Toddler Behavior Impacts Toddler

Discipline

The emotional changes that a toddler goes through can be wild and unpredictable. This is the reason that toddlers often act out—they do not know how to handle the emotions inside them. When you consider toddler behavior, it is important to look at it with empathy. It is not a firm hand that is needed during these times—but an empathetic approach that teaches a toddler how to handle their experiences. You should be loving and guiding, rather than strict and distant.

Benefits of Creating a Toddler Discipline Strategy

Something to keep in mind as you read this book is that you will need to adjust the discipline strategy that you use based on your own child's habits and responses to your discipline. By observing how the different methods work with your child, you will be able to come up with a toddler discipline strategy. The benefits of developing this include:

- Consistency- When you are consistent with what you expect of your toddler, and the resulting disciplinary action, you send a strong, clear message. Your toddler starts to associate certain behaviors with the discipline that results. Additionally, they learn what behaviors make you pleased with them.
- Clear Expectations- The consistency that is created with a well-thought-out strategy gives your toddler clear expectations to

live up to. They know what they can and cannot do and learn the difference between wrong and write. This is advantageous because it will encourage better decision making and behavior from your toddler in the future.

- Self-Control- When you create a strategy for toddler discipline, it helps your toddler learn what behaviors are and are not acceptable. As you help them learn to label and manage the emotions they are feeling, it promotes better self-control and good mental health.
- Decision-Making- Something that we must do as parents is teach our children how to thrive later in life. We will not always be there to make decision for them, nor

should we be. As your toddler shows their individuality and their capability for making decisions, it is important to guide them in a positive way. When a strategy is applied correctly, it helps shape the adolescent, then the adult, that your toddler will grow into and the decisions they will make later in life.

- Communication- One of the most important things about your relationship with your child is proper communication. Having an open channel of communication will let your toddler express him- or herself to you, without the fear of judgment. This leads to a better relationship in the future, hopefully one that will carry

through your child's teenage years.
- Improved Behavior- All these factors lead to better behavior for your toddler. They learn to properly express their needs and emotions and poor behavior decreases as a result. You will no longer feel as stressed and your toddler will be much happier, or at least able to express and manage their rough times.

Observing and Understanding Your Toddler's Behavior

Coming up with a discipline strategy for your toddler is not something that you can do or implement overnight. It takes patience and time because you are creating positive and healthy habits for your toddler. The very first step is to learn more about your toddler and how/why they behave. Follow these steps to observe and understand your child's behavior, so you can discipline them appropriately.

1. Observe Your Child as They Play, Sleep, and Eat- As a parent, you are always watching your child to some extent. Instead of looking for signs of trouble, however, spend your time watching them as they go about their day. Spend a couple days observing your child's behavior and looking for patterns that may indicate what areas need to be addressed. For example, you may notice that your toddler hides in the corner when he/she is frustrated. This would indicate that you need to talk to them

more about managing frustration. While taking a 'time out' from the activity by hiding is a great sign of a little self-control, you may need to address having your toddler share their feelings more.

2. Talk to Your Toddler- A critical part of proper discipline is having an open relationship with your toddler when it comes to communication. One of the biggest bad habits that parents get into is shaming their toddler for their behavior or showing too much disappointment. This discourages them and causes them to want to hide their emotions, which can cause serious emotional problems later. Instead, keep the channels of communication open. Rather than asking vague questions like "How was play time?" or "Did you have fun at preschool today?", ask about what

they built with their building blocks or how their art project went at preschool. Being specific will help your toddler communicate better.

3. Learn to be Empathetic- Spend a day thinking about what you would do if you were in your child's shoes. Try to label his or her emotions as they happen, by observing the situation and the behaviors that result. Consider what they may be thinking or feeling in that moment. Then, think about how you feel when you are experiencing the same emotion. By being compassionate to how your child feels, you will better be able to respond to their needs and decide when discipline is needed.

4. Identify Problem Areas- As you observe your child, you are going to notice problem areas that must be

addressed. Jot down the repetitive behavioral problems that you see. You will use this information later as you set boundaries and rules for your child. For example, you may use the three worst offenses as those that will put your toddler in time out.

5. Evaluate Your Toddler's Environment- Toddlers are sponges. Something else that you must consider as you think of a disciplinary plan is the role models that your child has in their life. Do they have an older sibling or a caregiver with a bad habit they may be picking up on? For example, does your toddler's yelling when they are frustrated remind you of the way one of their parent acts when angry? It is important to remember how impressionable toddlers are—they are

not the only ones responsible for the way that they behave.

6. Schedule Plenty of Quality Time- The economy today leaves many households with two working parents, meaning that children get to spend less time with the people who should care for them most. Even when work seems to get in the way, it is important to schedule quality time with your toddler. Interacting with them one-on-one will boost your relationship and show them how much you care. It also fosters positive communication and gives you a better chance to observe your child and their emotions as they happen.

CHAPTER SUMMARY:

1. Toddlers are at a pivotal and stressful

moment in their lives, as they experience a wider range of emotion and learn more about the world. To understand your toddler's behaviors, you must be aware of some of the most common reasons for poor behavior choices. Toddlers often misbehave because they do not know how to express or manage emotions, lack self-control, are over stimulated, have a need that is not being met, want attention, or are just having a bad day. By narrowing down the problem, you can respond with an appropriate disciplinary action.

2. Before you begin using the advice in this book to discipline your toddler, you should sit down and come up with a toddler discipline strategy. This is important because it creates consistency, makes expectations known,

improves self-control and decision-making, fosters communication with your toddler, and improves behavior overall.

3. Before you can develop a strategy for disciplining your toddler, you must understand them and why they behave the way they do. Observing your child can be very helpful for this. Pay attention to how they behave playing, sleeping, and during meal times and encourage them to communicate with you. You can also learn more about appropriate disciplinary strategies by identifying problem areas, sympathizing with your child's emotions, considering their environment, and scheduling quality time with your toddler.

YOUR QUICK START ACTION STEP: CONSIDER YOUR CHILD'S BEHAVIOR

Right now, consider a behavioral habit that your toddler would like to stop. Research this behavior and a plan of discipline. This will give you practice on observing and understanding your toddler's behavior. Once you understand the reasoning behind what they are doing, you will be able to act more appropriately.

Chapter 3: Effective Communication: How to Connect with your Child

Chapter 3: Effective Communication: How to Connect with your Child

Effective communication and empathy go hand-in-hand when it comes to disciplining a toddler. When your toddler is struggling, they are going to look to you for guidance. It is important that you give them the chance to express themselves and learn how they are feeling. Then, you can respond with the proper discipline or redirection, to encourage better behavior in the future.

Toddler Discipline and Effective Communication

We have all been there. We have had a

long day at home or a terrible day at work and the first thing we want to do when we get home is talk to a friend or our spouse. We express how the day made us feel and share what made us so upset. Toddlers, unfortunately, do not yet have the ability to describe the emotions that they are experiencing. This means that when your toddler cannot get his toy to turn on for the sixth time in a row and he chucks it across the room, it is only because he lacks the skills to communicate his frustration. Had he communicated, you may have helped your toddler figure out the toy—before it smashed into several pieces against the wall.

When it comes to toddler communication, effective communication means a few things.

First, effective communication means that you have considered your toddler's behavior by considering how they are feeling at the time and how they might better be able to channel that emotion. Second, it means that you can speak about emotions and what your toddler is feeling with them. This 'labeling' is important because identifying what he or she is feeling will help your toddler express his or her feelings. Finally, effective communication means that you can help your toddler differentiate between good choices and poor choices. This involves helping your toddler learn the difference between right and wrong, as well as what is deemed acceptable and unacceptable by society.

Do not fret if you have not yet developed effective toddler communication for the purpose of giving appropriate discipline. This chapter will go into depth about how to foster positive communication with your toddler that will improve their behavior.

Benefits of Effective Communication

When you effectively communicate with your toddler for the purpose of creating a positive discipline strategy, there are several benefits, including:

- Improved Parent-Child Relationship- As children become adolescents, they tend to push their parents away and cut off communication. To help prevent this, it is important to nurture positive communication with your child as a toddler. By communicating effectively and without shaming them, you are teaching your toddler that they can come to you for anything—something that will be carried over into their adolescent years if you remain consistent.

- Increased Ability to Identify Emotions- When your toddler learns that they can come to you with problems, they will start to come to you when they are experiencing unpleasant emotions. It is important to always address these as being natural. Help your child redirect the emotion or let them talk to you about what is upsetting them.
- Better Problem-Solving Skills- Toddlers that communicate their

emotions effectively have completed the first step to problem solving—identifying the problem. When your child comes to you with an emotional problem, talk them through it. By brainstorming what the child can do, you nurture their ability to solve problems on their own.

- Emotional Regulation- Parents who communicate effectively with their toddlers will find that their son/daughter can regulate their emotions better. This is a skill that will be very useful later in life as well, especially once your toddler must deal with the throes of adolescents in ten years.
- Teaches Empathy- When you communicate well with your toddler, they are learning that

you care for them and how they are feeling. This models empathy, an important characteristic for your child to develop for healthy social relationships.

How to Establish Effective Communication for Toddler Discipline

1. Take a Moment Before You React- When you react to suddenly, you do not give yourself time to be empathetic or come up with a plan for discipline. Unless your child is in danger, think about how they may be feeling or the reason behind their behavior. Once you have done this, you can approach the child.

2. Get Down on Your Toddler's Level-

Do you remember how we discussed in the first chapter that yelling is not effective? This is especially true if you are across the room, away from your toddler. When your child is in trouble, it is critical that you do not yell at them unless they are in immediate danger and you need to get their attention. Walk to the child and talk to them. Some children have trouble paying attention and they may stare in another direction or space off. To keep them focused, get down on their level. You can also place your hand gently on their shoulder or ask them to hold your hand while you talk to them.

3. Don't Demand Eye Contact- You should never demand eye contact when your toddler is being lectured. Even when you get on their level, they may

hide their face because they feel ashamed. It is important that we do not embarrass them further and make them look at us while they are being reprimanded. Keep in mind that your toddler does not have to be looking at you to be listening. Maintain your hold on their hand or shoulder and engage them in the conversation to be sure they are listening.

4. Talk it Out- To foster communication with your child, you should allow them to speak about what happened as well. Listen to your toddler and what he or she was thinking at the time of the incident. Encourage them to share their feelings and what they believe was happening non-judgmentally. This will let you gather information before you decide what to do next.

5. Identify the Problem- Once your toddler has described the situation to you, help them identify the problem that got them in trouble. For example, if your child threw their toy, then you would explain that the feeling (anger or frustration) was not the problem—it was how they reacted to that feeling (by throwing the toy).

6. Find a Better Solution Together- Once your toddler understands what went wrong, you can help them think of a solution. Give them a chance to explain what they could do differently next time. If they cannot think of anything, guide them in coming up with a better solution. Returning to the example of throwing the toy, the toddler could have asked for help instead or taken a break from the toy that was making him or her

upset.

7. Discipline if Necessary- Once you understand the situation and have talked to your toddler, decide if further discipline is needed. For most first offenses, it is sometimes best to tell the toddler what will happen if the problem persists. The next time that they repeat the behavior, discipline them in an appropriate way and remind them what they should be doing instead.

CHAPTER SUMMARY:

1. Effective communication is a critical tool in toddler discipline. If you do not talk to your toddler and do not understand how they are feeling, you cannot give them the guidance they need to deal with their emotions. Without

proper communication, your child may continue to have behavioral problems because they cannot form the relationships between consequences and their behaviors.

2. There are a number of benefits to effective communication when it comes to discipline, including a better parent-child relationship, the ability to label and regulate emotions, improved problem-solving skills, and learned empathy.

3. It is never too late to start fostering healthy and effective communication with your toddler. By taking steps including thinking the situation through, getting down on your toddler's level, discussing the problem with them, and helping them problem solve before turning to discipline, you can encourage

your child's development into a well-rounded adult.

YOUR QUICK START ACTION STEP: START COMMUNICATING WITH YOUR CHILD

Even though we have not gotten into the specific of discipline (that is coming in the next chapter), now is a good time to put the above communication strategy into practice. In addition to following through with this communication when your child misbehaves, be sure to engage with them when they are doing good as well. Encourage them to talk to you about their day and feelings regularly, to show that you are supportive and understanding of the emotions they may be dealing with. If you are especially busy or have trouble taking time out of your schedule to do this, set time aside in your schedule especially for communicating with your toddler. If you are not close to them, it may be the source of their bad behavior.

Chapter 4: Discipline Strategies

Chapter 4: Discipline Strategies

Troublesome toddler behavior can happen anywhere. However, there are some places and situations where toddler misbehavior is more common. In this chapter, we will focus on the most common places and situations when your toddler may need discipline to make the right behavioral choices. These strategies will be specific and helpful—as well as based on techniques that you can feel comfortable using without any stress or guilt.

Why You Need Specific Discipline Strategies

As mentioned before, consistency with your child is key to discipline success. By developing specific strategies, you ensure you remain consistent with consequences and the behaviors that you expect from your toddler. This is critical for toddler discipline success. Here are some benefits of using a variety of discipline strategies to encourage good behavior from your toddler:

- Consistency Among Caregivers- Many parents are not fortunate enough to be home with their toddler for most of the day. When there is more than one caregiver, a toddler can easily become confused about what is expected by each one. This causes misbehavior. When you have set strategies that you use for specific places and situations, all caregivers can refer to the guidelines as they discipline the toddler. This united approach will improve child behavior quicker.

- Lowered Stress Levels- Sometimes, a toddler's behavior can leave their parent wanting to pull their hair out. When you have a strategy for your child's behavioral problems, you can feel more in control in the situation. As an added benefit, your toddler will notice your collectedness and are more likely to accept that you are in charge.
- Targeted Approach to Discipline- Toddler discipline is not a one-size-fits-all approach. It is highly important that you consider your child's individuality as you choose

the proper discipline based on the place or scenario. Some techniques will work better for some children than others. Even so, when you apply different techniques based on the specifics of the situation, you can find what works best and then implement it as part of your strategy.

Discipline Strategies for Places

In Public

When your child misbehaves in public, it quickly becomes a stressful situation for everyone involved. Some parents give into their toddlers in these moments, believing that it is best to get everyone's eyes off them as quickly as possible. If you do not want to encourage these behaviors, however, you must take the following steps:

1. Start by talking to your child about expectations beforehand. Any time that you take your child in public, you should set rules for expected behavior. If you take him or her to the park, for example, your rules may be that they cannot fight with other children and that when you say it is time to go, they cannot argue. In the grocery store, the rules may be that they are not allowed to wander away from their parent or touch anything. Set 2-3 rules and tell them what the consequences will be if they cannot follow them.

2. If your child does not listen, respond quickly by giving them quiet time. This

is usually done by keeping them near you. For example, you could find a bench to have them sit down on with you or you can have them stand between you and the cart while they are in quiet time. Then, allow them to go back to walking regularly once the time is up.

3. If they continue not to listen or they throw a fit over quiet time, remove your toddler from the area. Have them sit outside or away from the action with you for a few minutes and decide if it is okay for them to return once you have talked about the problem and what is expected of them.

At Bedtime

Bedtime behavior can be a struggle, especially if your toddler is over-tired or over stimulated from a long day. You should avoid punishments at bedtime because it creates negative emotions toward going to sleep that will cause more problems in the future.

1. One strategy that you should implement before your toddler goes to bed is to develop a routine. For my children, this involves each of them watching one episode of a show that they pick and then brushing teeth. We share a story and have bedtime cuddles, they get half a cup of water, and they go to sleep. Once you do develop a regular bedtime routine with your toddler, be sure that any caregivers or babysitters are aware of your child's bedtime routine. Otherwise, your toddler may give them a hard time.

2. If there is something specific that you are struggling with at bedtime, sit down

and discuss expectations with your child. Gentle guidance is best in this time because punishing your child when they are already tired will just yield negative results. Also, be empathetic toward your child during this time, as they may be having problems because they are overly tired.

3. If your child always asks for a small cup of water before bed, start getting it ready beforehand. Some toddlers will postpone bedtime by asking for extra trips to the bathroom or more water. Have a pre-set schedule and make your child adhere to it every night. This consistency with rules will teach him/her what is expected at bedtime and they will give you fewer problems in the future.

Dinner Table/During Meal Time

If poor dinner table behavior is a problem, you will need to use a targeted approach. Addressing this problem at home is critical because the habits that your toddler learns at home will be carried over to daycare, school, family member's homes, and restaurants. Therefore, it is essential that you teach them not to throw food and to use good table manners.

Consequences can be useful for misbehavior during mealtime. Setting expectations is important as well. Here are some strategies you can use.

1. Start by establishing some dinnertime rules for at your home that everyone is required to follow. This includes things like using your silverware when you eat, sitting with the family while eating, or any other things that your toddler

struggles with. Setting rules clarifies expectations for your child, so they are more likely to rise to the occasion and do what you ask them to.

2. As you establish rules, you must also establish consequences. Decide how you are going to respond to your toddler when they misbehave at dinnertime, but keep in mind that you do not want to give them what they want. You can remove them and have them sit in quiet time until they are ready to behave or take them to time out if they will not be quiet. If throwing food is the problem, make your child pick up their mess. However, this may not be a good idea for toddlers who choose to throw their food because they want attention or because they do not want to eat what they have been given. Regardless of the

disciplinary action you choose for each of these scenarios, be consistent.

In the Car

Toddler behavior in the car can become distracting, which is a danger when you are trying to focus on driving. This makes quick action critical to prevent a stressful situation. There are a few techniques that you can use in the car, depending on what works with your child. This includes taking a privilege away from your child or creating another logical consequence. Another great choice is the 'energy drain' trick, which is described here.

1. Address the problem- For example, "I cannot focus on driving while you are fighting with your brother. It is draining my energy."

2. Follow with a Consequence- "If I do not have enough energy, I will not be able to play with you when we get home" or "I will not be able to take you to the park."

At Daycare

Daycares have a responsibility of caring for your children. They often use time out or remove kids from the situation, usually to talk to them about their feelings. If it is a serious enough issue, they will often talk to you when you pick your toddler up from daycare. In some cases, you may want to address the problem to reinforce the ideas that they learned after being disciplined by the daycare worker.

1. You should start by allowing your toddler the chance to tell you about what

happened while they were at daycare. Remember to keep an open mind. It is okay to bring up the topic if they do not—but you should not do it in a way that can be perceived as threatening or punishing.

2. After the situation has been brought up, ask them to share how they were feeling at the time or what caused them to behave it. Then, come up with ways to solve the problem in the future.

3. Always remember that unless the behavior is severe, it does not require the idea to be drilled into your child's head or for them to be punished again. You can address it, but do so in a way that is conversational and encourages your child to share.

Discipline Strategies for

Situations for a Child Who...

Hits

Your first reaction when your child hits you or someone else may be to hit them back. Unfortunately, when you hit your toddler, you are sending the message that hitting is okay and encouraging their aggressive behavior. Hitting is something where logical or natural consequences may not work as well. You need to remove your child from the situation and give them time to reflect.

1. Before you resort to time out, give your child the option of quiet time. Quiet time happens in the same area of the incident. Your child is not isolated. You sit with them while they are in quiet time for a set amount of time. Then, if they do well, you will talk to them about the problem (hitting) and that it means

they are frustrated or angry. Help them come up with a solution to the problem.

2. If your child protests quiet time or will not sit quietly, remove him or her to another room. This should be a designated spot in your home. However, to prevent negative associations, you should not make the time out area your child's bedroom.

3. Decide on the time that your child will be sitting in time out. Their time out does not start until they are quiet. As soon as it is up, spend time talking to your child about hitting, why they cannot do it, and better outlets for the emotions that your toddler was feeling at the time.

Screams

Redirection is a good tool when your

child is screaming. This is especially true if they are screaming because of an encounter with another child or because they are frustrated. Rather than punishing them, redirect their attention to another activity.

1. Start by identifying the reason they are screaming and remove the object or remove them from the situation. Explain calmly that you are removing them or the object because they are angry/frustrated.

2. Next, get your toddler involved with something else. By saying, "Let's go get a cup of juice" or "Let's find a new toy to play with," you are giving your child the tool they need to walk away and do something else when they are frustrated or angry. This will become critical as they learn emotional regulation and self-

control.

3. If suggesting something to your toddler does not work, try giving them a task to do instead. For example, if they are screaming in the supermarket and redirection does not work, ask them to help you buy groceries. Let them pick the things they can reach off the shelves and put them in the basket. By keeping them engaged, you are encouraging helpfulness and keeping their mind focused, so they are less likely to have a meltdown.

Refuses to Eat

Refusing to eat is a common toddler behavior. Whether they 'don't' like it' or would rather be doing something else, it becomes problematic if your child is not getting the nutrition they need.

However, note that not eating the foods you put in front of them is a common problem with toddlers. There are a few strategies that you can consider for this, but you should not really punish your child. You do not want to create negative emotions and pair them with eating.

1. If your child never eats dinner, then chances are, they will not want to eat most nights. Try putting something that they will eat on their plates if you are worried about them being hungry. This could be a slice of bread served alongside whatever you are eating. If they continue to only eat the bread to fill their stomach, this can become a problem, so vary the things that you offer them.

2. Something else that you should do is make a big deal about the food and how

good it tastes. Encourage your toddler to at least try the food—not even to eat it. Sometimes, getting them to put the food in their mouth and realize that it is tasty is the only missing step between a toddler that eats and one who does not.

3. If you know that your child does not like the food that they are being served, meaning they have tried it and it does not suit their taste buds, ask your toddler about why they do not like it, so you can make food more suited to their taste buds in the future. If you are serving something for dinner they do not like, give them a few options that they can choose from. By creating choices, they have the option of choosing something they like to eat, but you remain in control.

4. Odds are, your toddler is not going to

starve. Give them a multivitamin to make sure they are getting enough nutrition and speak to your toddler's doctor if you are worried. If you want to give them a snack before bed, be sure it is unrelated to the dinner incident before.

5. If your child does not eat their food that they asked for, you can refuse to offer something else until they eat what was asked for. This is especially useful for daytime snacking, especially if your toddler tends to ask for things to eat and then smashes them or leaves them laying around. Explain the importance of not wasting food and put the snack on a table until your child is hungry enough to eat it.

Throws Things

Depending on what your child is throwing and if they are in danger because of it, you may want to let a natural consequence unfold. For example, if they throw they toy against the wall and it breaks, they have learned that if they throw their toys, they cannot play with them anymore. Alternatively, you can take the child's toy away as a form of logical consequence or place them in time out. To take away the toy, do the following.

1. Tell your child firmly to give you the toy. Explain that they threw it and now you are going to take it away and put it up for a designated amount of time. You can take away the toy for an hour or for a full day, but you should not stretch the punishment longer than this because your toddler will no longer form the

association between throwing the toy and losing it.

2. If your child will not give you the toy willingly, you should not give them the attention they are demanding by chasing them or taking it by force. If they will not give it to you, threaten them with quiet time or time out. Remind them that even if they give you a hard time, they will still lose the toy.

3. Once you have the toy, put it up where your child cannot reach it. If they did not give it up willingly, follow through with quiet time or time out.

CHAPTER SUMMARY:

1. You should not have to stress or feel guilty to discipline your toddler. The strategies discussed in this chapter will

help you do just this—in any situation that may arise.

2. By coming up with a plan for discipline, you create the consistency that your toddler needs to form connections between the behavioral decision and the resulting consequence. You also shape your expectations, lower stress levels, create appropriate disciplinary plans, create a strategy that all caregivers can use effectively, and use a targeted and effective approach to disciplinary situations.

3. There is more than one way to discipline a toddler in certain scenarios. By applying the techniques discussed in this chapter and the ideas for discipline provided in the first chapter, you can come up with a strategy that will be effective in getting your toddler to

behave the way you want them to.

YOUR QUICK START ACTION STEP: CREATE A STRATEGY OUTLINE

There are many aspects of discipline that you will want to remember. In this step, outline some problem behaviors for your child and how you want to respond. This serves the purpose of keeping you consistent, especially since the disciplinary strategies applied are likely different from the ones you are currently using. Creating an outline and sharing it with other caregivers can also keep them consistent when it comes to appropriately disciplining your toddler.

Chapter 5: Stressed Out? How to Remain Calm

Chapter 5: Stressed Out? How to Remain Calm

It can seem nearly impossible to keep your cool in the heat of the moment. Our natural reaction when children get loud is to get louder, by yelling or to get physical, by hitting. In these times, it is important to remember that the way that we react greatly impacts the behaviors that our toddler exhibits. Additionally, by reacting to the tantrum, we are giving the toddler the attention that they want—for all the wrong reasons.

It is natural that your child is going to rebel, especially if the discipline strategies discussed here are not ones that you use already. As you try to communicate and discipline, expect your toddler to fight back. It is important to remember that this will not last forever and by staying calm, your toddler will learn that their bad behavior does not phase you—nor does it get them what they want.

Why You Need to Keep Your Cool

Imagine that you were standing in the office of the President and he is asking you for political advice. That would be absurd, right? You may lose confidence in him and question his ability to do his job if he is asking someone with limited knowledge about politics and international relations to give their advice on a situation.

When it comes to your child, you are the

president. Your toddler looks to you as someone who will protect them from danger, catch them if they fall, and be there when they need help. If you yell or lose your composure, they are going to question your ability to lead. When you do stay cool, calm, and collected, however, you reap the following benefits:

- It Proves Your Credibility as a Leader- Your child looks to you as the leader of the home. They will respect your authority, but only if they feel confident in your abilities to handle stressful situations. Being calm will show that you know what you are doing and your toddler will look to you when they are feeling unsure of their feelings or what is happening around them.

- You Can Focus on Effective Discipline- When you learn to keep your cool when disciplining your child, you can think much more clearly. This gives you the ability to implement strategies, rather than giving into the stress of the situation.
- Discipline Becomes Stress-Free- Becoming overwhelmed creates unnecessary stress that can leave you frazzled, exhausted, and wondering why after an encounter with your toddler. As you learn effective strategies for discipline, you will be able to handle problems without worrying about what you possibly

can do to curb your toddler's behavior.

- You Will Not Feel Guilty After Disciplining Your Child- Sometimes, when parents lose their cool, they can feel guilty after an encounter with their toddler. This is especially true if they are too loud or spank the child because these are often ineffective methods that leave you questioning your skills as a parent.
- Home Becomes a Positive Environment Where Your Toddler Can Thrive- Toddlers respond well to calm, logical discipline. When you are calm, your child looks to you as support. You can guide them to make good behavioral choices

and to handle their emotions in an appropriate manner. In this way, they are surrounded by the positive feelings and guidance that they need to thrive.

How to Use Positive Discipline When Your Child is Throwing a Tantrum

If your child is throwing a tantrum, the first thing you should do is assess the situation for danger. Consider if they are at risk for harming themselves and if not, let them throw the tantrum for a moment. Use this time to calm yourself, using deep breathing or counting. If you cannot relax over the sounds of your child's tantrum, walk away for a few moments.

Many times, once a child realizes that

you simply are not responding to their tantrum, they will stop on their own. Once this happens, talk to them calmly about the situation and what emotions they were experiencing at the time. Then, help them problem solve as to what they could have done differently.

Often, temper tantrums result from a child not getting what they want. Be sure to explain that when your child acts that way, you cannot support their behavior by giving them what they want. Once they are doing the opposite behavior, be sure to provide positive reinforcement with your praise.

For example, imagine that one of your children has a toy and the other one tries to take it. When the second child is successful, the first throws a fit. When you take the toy away from the second child, they throw a tantrum.

With the second child, they should be removed to time out for taking the toy before you address the problem and how it can better be solved in the future. For example, you may walk them through scenarios where they ask the other child if they can share. Explain that if the child says no, they will not share, it is still not okay to take the toy. Instead, they should ask the other kid if they can have a turn once they have finished with the toy.

To handle the first child appropriately, you should return the toy that is taken. Before doing this, however, it is important to explain that throwing a tantrum does not solve problems. Instead, they should get an adult to handle the situation.

If you find yourself becoming overwhelmed, do not be afraid to walk away from the situation altogether. Be sure your child is safe first, then give yourself time to evaluate the situation. Think about how your toddler may be feeling and the cause of their behavior before reacting. This gives you time to logically consider the situation and respond appropriately, without yelling and without hitting.

CHAPTER SUMMARY:

1. Toddlers will naturally rebel as they start to learn the boundaries of the world around them. By keeping calm, you can implement a discipline strategy that comes without stress, without guilt, and with a high rate of effectiveness.

2. There are numerous benefits of staying calm when you are disciplining your toddler. Having a calm demeanor will make discipline stress- and guilt-free, as well as assure your child of your authority and create a positive environment where your child can thrive.

3. It is okay, even encouraged, for you to walk away when you become overwhelmed with your toddler's behavior. By taking a deep breath or counting and giving yourself time to consider the situation, you make it more likely that you will choose an appropriate disciplinary solution. It is possible to deal with tantrums without hitting or yelling—you just have to have the clarity of mind to do it.

YOUR QUICK START ACTION STEP: USE ONE OF THE TIPS TO COOL YOURSELF IN TIMES OF STRESS

The next time that your child is throwing a fit, use one of the strategies above to help yourself approach the situation calm and collected. Not only will you show your authority in the face of stress, you make it much more likely that your child will choose to listen to you.

Chapter 6: Common Mistakes and How to Avoid Them

Chapter 6: Common Mistakes and How to Avoid Them

In this chapter, we will discuss some of the most common mistakes that parents make when disciplining a toddler. It is very easy to make these mistakes—and the first step is identifying problem areas.

Common Mistakes When Disciplining a Toddler

1. Bribery- Bribery can be an effective method of getting your toddler to do what you want—but only in that moment. There may be times when

misbehaving is a lot more fun than the piece of candy you are offering for good behavior. Other times, your child just may not feel like listening to you. When you bribe, you also create an expectation that your toddler is only behaving to earn something. If you want them to behave consistently, it is important that you do not constantly give them gifts for good behavior.

2. Not Listening- As a parent, you want your child to give you their full attention when you discipline them. The problem is that some parents do not give their full attention when their toddler is speaking. Remember that you must lead by example. If your toddler is communicating with you, turn off the television, do not pick up your phone, and give them the attention and respect

that you want them to give you when they are being addressed.

3. Lack of Patience- Parents who try to implement disciplinary strategies may give up after a week, feeling like it is not working on their children. Something that you must remember, however, is that your child's behavior is not going to change overnight. Discipline is a constant process that is going to change with age. While your toddler's behavior will eventually improve overall, it is critical that you put a full effort into the changes that you want to see. If you give up too soon, then the strategies will not have a chance to work.

4. Expecting Too Much- First-time parents especially do not have a good idea of what their children are capable of. Sometimes, we expect better

behavior from our toddler, but do not take the time to understand what the root of the issue is. When you expect too much, you set your child up for failure. Instead, offer guidance in these situations so your child learns what you expect. For example, if you do not want them running around the house on a nice day, consider taking them outside. They obviously need an outlet or a better way to redirect their energy. You cannot expect them to be still when they are full of energy.

5. Being Inconsistent- Inconsistency will confuse your toddler and make them unsure of what you expect. This leads to poor behavior later, as they push boundaries to try and define their independence and their place in the world. Additionally, inconsistency

among caregivers can be a problem for the same reason. Your child may push boundaries with one person while behaving well for another.

Benefits of Identifying Mistakes

Before you can start correcting parent mistakes, you must know what you are doing wrong. It can be hard to look at our parenting style with a critical eye, especially when we are worried we have not been compassionate enough with our child. Keep in mind, however, that those are the mistakes of the past and by learning from them, you can start shaping a positive future for your toddler.

- Chance to Correct Them- It is never too late to adopt new parenting strategies and start guiding your child, rather than punishing them. Regardless of your child's age, you can implement new strategies now and with time, they will become the norm. The only way to know which of your discipline methods need replaced is to know which mistakes you are making.
- Reduced Guilt and Stress- When parents feel stressed or guilty after an encounter with their child, it is often caused by making a parenting mistake. By identifying mistakes and learning to avoid them, you can make a more positive experience for you

and your toddler—one that you both feel better after.

- Better Relationship with Your Toddler- When you care enough about your toddler's well-being to identify and alter parenting mistakes, you are working toward improving your relationship. They will start to look at you as someone that should be respected for guidance, rather than feared out of authority.

How to Avoid Common Parenting Mistakes

1. Identifying the Mistakes- After reading through this chapter, you may already know a few things you are doing wrong. Remember that this is not a time to judge yourself—but to encourage learning and betterment. Becoming a

better parent is something that will improve your life and the life of your toddler's, so it is well worth it.

2. Evaluate Your Emotions- How do you feel after disciplining your toddler? Do you feel confident that you have given them the foundation they need for emotional regulation and problem solving, or do you feel shameful or guilty about your tactics afterward? A little self-doubt is okay, but if you are overly stressed or guilty about what transpired, you may want to evaluate your technique for mistakes.

3. Evaluate Your Child's Emotions- Your toddler will respond better when you use a positive parenting approach. If your child seems saddened or angry after your encounter, there may be some unresolved issues that need addressed.

4. Be Prepared to Accept Criticism- Sometimes, the biggest thing standing in the way when you try to implement a new parenting strategy is yourself. It can be hard to evaluate your own strategies, especially if you are already doubting your abilities as a parent. Remember that the goal is to make a better life for your child. It does not matter what happened in the past—it matters what you do now.

CHAPTER SUMMARY:

1. The most common mistakes that parents make is using bribery to get their toddler to behave, not listening to their child, losing patience too quickly, expecting too much, and being inconsistent.

2. By identifying common mistakes that parents make when disciplining, you can evaluate your own strategies and make adjustments where needed. This offers the benefits of giving you the chance to correct problems, reduced guilt and stress, and a better relationship with your toddler.

3. By making the necessary steps, you can ensure you are implementing better parenting strategies. You can do this by knowing the most common parenting mistakes, evaluating your emotions and the emotions of your toddler, and being prepared to accept criticism in a constructive way.

YOUR QUICK START ACTION STEP: IDENTIFY COMMON

PARENTING MISTAKES

For the next step, consider other areas of parenting that you feel stressed or guilty over. Then, do some research to find out if you are doing something wrong. By doing this, you give yourself the tools to better care for your toddler's disciplinary needs. As you evaluate what is wrong with your strategies, be sure to look up tips on how to correct these problem areas.

Chapter 7: How to Discipline a Special Needs Child

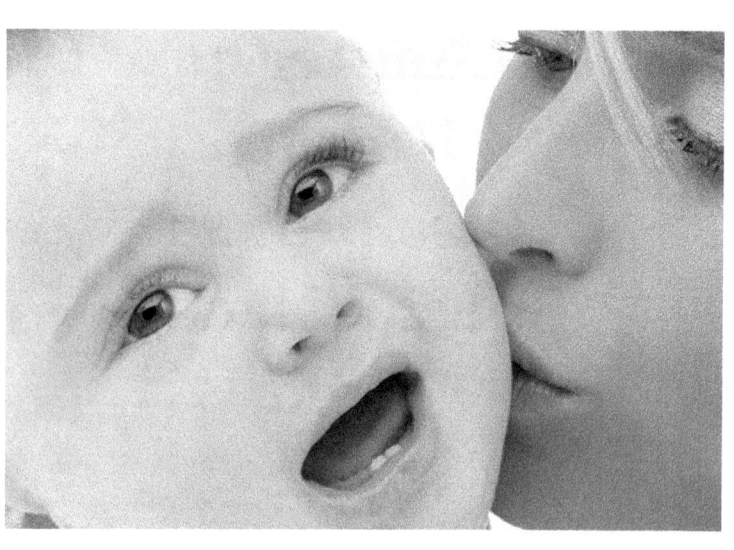

Chapter 7: How to Discipline a Special Needs Child

One of the emotions that parents often experience when they are raising a special needs child is stress. They constantly worry if what they are doing is right, even more so than the average parent. The good news is that what you have learned so far will provide a good basis for what you need to know to discipline a child with special needs and this chapter will teach you about the differences. It is possible to discipline your special needs child without guilt or stress—you just have to know how.

Benefits of Using a Unique Disciplinary Approach for Your Special Needs Child

Special needs children do not always have the ability to make the same associations in their mind as the average toddler. This does not mean that they are not intelligent. In fact, most special needs children are very smart—they just lack the connections needed to communicate well and respond to a regular disciplinary regimen. When you do find a method of discipline that works for your special needs child, you will experience the following benefits:

- Better Understanding of Your Child's Needs- As you teach your special needs toddler to understand their emotions, they will better be able to communicate their needs. In this instance, learning to listen to body language, not just words, is important. Be receptive to what your toddler is trying to communicate, even when they cannot find the right words.

- Improved Empathy- As you learn your child's special emotional needs, your empathy towards them will improve. This alone can improve your parenting efforts because you understand them better. Researching your toddler's condition can be especially helpful in this regard.

- Improved Emotional Regulation- Like with disciplining the average toddler, choosing the right methods is going to help your special needs toddler regulate their emotions. This is incredibly beneficial since many of their social and learning disabilities come from an inability to understand and manage their emotions.

Meeting the Special Needs of Your Child: Discipline for ADHD and Autism

Two of the most common mental illness that affect children are ADHD and Autism. This section will provide an example of gentle, but effective methods you can use.

ADHD

The major problem that children with ADHD have is that they cannot focus. Sometimes, they also make poor behavioral choices because they are overwhelmed by stimuli or bored with their environment. The key, therefore, is helping them learn to find the balance between these areas and focus in on what they should be doing at the time.

With children that have ADHD, you should expect to repeat yourself—even more than you would with the average toddler. Redirection is also an incredibly useful tool when children with ADHD become upset. By refocusing their energy and having them focus it elsewhere, it can eliminate problems.

Simplicity and routine are also incredibly beneficial for children with ADHD. Routines help your child learn what to expect, so they can focus at key points during the say. Simplicity is also important as you discuss rules and consequences—being too complex or using lengthy explanations will cause your child to misunderstand your or become distracted.

Finally, you will need to keep a close, watchful eye over your ADHD child. Their short attention span can cause them to misbehave or wander off if they become distracted by something.

Autism

One of the biggest obstacles you will need to overcome with your autistic child is communication. Rather than teaching them to communicate as you would, you must learn what types of communication work best for your autistic child. Use many methods of communication, including visual cues, gestures, written language, and verbal communication. You should also start with short, easy-to-understand sentences and slowly advance them.

Positivity is another big factor for autistic children. Be sure to state the behaviors that you want—rather than the ones that you do not want. Focusing on the positives will yield misbehavior. You should also constantly praise your child when they do something well, helping to form that connection between good behaviors and the good feeling that they get from praise.

Routines and schedules are also important for autistic children. This puts them at ease because they know what to expect throughout the day. This familiarity will encourage good behavior.

CHAPTER SUMMARY:

1. Special needs children require a slightly different style of parenting than most. It can be easy to become frustrated, but by developing a discipline strategy, you can improve the behavior of any toddler.

2. There are several benefits of choosing appropriate discipline methods for your special needs child. These include improved empathy, better communication, and a better understanding of your child's needs.

3. Two of the most common behavioral problems of children are ADHD and Autism. Both types of children benefit from a targeted approach that includes simplicity, routine, and proper

discipline. You should also keep a watchful eye on your child and avoid physical punishment.

YOUR QUICK START ACTION STEP: LEARN MORE ABOUT SPECIAL NEEDS DISCPLINE

One of the best things you can do for your special needs child is get educated. Instead of stressing, do some research to learn more about how to discipline your child. The techniques will vary slightly from what has been learned prior to this chapter, but as a whole, the positive parenting approach can be very beneficial.

BONUS Chapter: When Strategies don't seem to Work

BONUS Chapter: When Strategies don't seem to Work

While the ideal situation would be that every parent who read this book would implement the strategies and find success, there will be times when what you have learned just seems like it is not working. In these situations, it is important to keep your calm. Rather than hitting or yelling, try out the strategies in this chapter.

Why You Need to Tweak Disciplinary Approaches

While this book has been created with the intention of helping parents become better disciplinarians, it is important to remember that there is no manual for parenting. Every child is unique and a strategy that works for one child may not work for another. Fortunately, with a little tweaking, you can easily change your disciplinary approach to reap the following benefits:

- Learning What Your Child Needs- The good news is that once you find a discipline strategy that works, it is likely to keep working. As you provide consistent methods, your toddler will learn to adapt to your needs.
- You Can Make Appropriate Adjustments- By analyzing your current methods and deciding what works and does not work, you can begin to make

adjustments that work. This lets you discipline your child without feeling stressed or guilty.

- Your Toddler Will Behave Better- When you adjust based on your toddler's unique needs and personality, you will find a method that makes them behave. It is important to remember that yelling and hitting are not good options—there are many other tactics out there to try when you become frustrated.

What to Do When Your Child...

Doesn't Respond to Discipline Efforts

If you are just starting to implement new

discipline efforts, then it is going to take time before your child gets the gist of the situation. Remember to be patient—it can take several weeks of using a specific tactic before it is effective.

If your child still is not responding to discipline efforts, try a new tactic. The first chapter provided you several methods to try. Give one that you have not attempted yet a chance and see if that helps curb your child's behavior. You can adapt it to fit your child's personality. For example, one child may respond better to taking away a privilege like riding their bike outside, while another may be encouraged to behave if you threaten to take away television.

Is Talking Back

Often, when your child talks back, it is

because they do not feel they are being listened to. Instead of lashing out through yelling, take the time to have a conversation with your toddler. Consider their thoughts and feelings and give them a chance to explain. After listening to them, explain yourself and why you want them to do what you have asked. If they remain unreasonable, implement a consequence for their non-listening behavior and follow through with it.

Does Not Listen

If your child refuses to listen, then evaluate what is going on around them. If the environment is too busy, remove your child to another room or shut off stimuli like music or the television. Then, get down on your child's level and have them hold your hand or touch their

2. When you tweak disciplinary actions to fit the needs of your toddler, you will reap many benefits, including learning what your child needs for better behavior, making adjustments to achieve that, and experiencing better behavior from your toddler as a result.

3. By following a series of steps when your child does not respond to your effort, talks back, or chooses not to listen, you can develop consistency and expectations. Your child will eventually learn what is expected and what will result if they choose not to listen.

YOUR QUICK START ACTION STEP: TROUBLESHOOT YOUR TODDLER'S PROBLEMS

If your child simply is not doing what

shoulder gently.

As you talk to them, ask them to tell you what you said. Do not expect them to parrot this information back to you. Instead, have them speak with their own words and consider what they think you mean and what you really mean. If there is a difference between these ideas, then the problem may not be that your child is not listening—the problem may be miscommunication.

CHAPTER SUMMARY:

1. Disciplinary strategies sometimes need adjusted for you to successfully discipline your child. This is because each toddler is an individual and the method that works for one may need to be adapted to work for another.

you want them to, take the time to implement one of the strategies addressed above. It is important to remember that discipline takes time, but if a strategy is not working, a new approach can be beneficial. Always take the time to understand your toddler and be sure miscommunication is not the root of the problem.

Conclusion

Thank you again for owning this book!

I hope this book was able to help you to become a better toddler parent, by teaching you to raise your little one with proper discipline. It can be hard to sort through all the misinformation and advice that is out their regarding children, but by reading this book, you have taken the first critical step to getting toddler discipline right.

The next step is to put your strategy into action. You can start communicating effectively with your toddler for discipline today. Through communication and observation, you can decide which strategies will be most effective. Then, tweak the strategies until you find something that works well for you and your child.

Finally, if this book has given you value and helped you in any way, then I'd like to ask you for a favor if you would be kind enough to leave a review for this book on Amazon? It'd be greatly appreciated!

Thank you and good luck!

Toddler Potty Training:

Incredibly Simple 2-Day Potty Training that Works

Marie C. Foster

© **Copyright 2018 by Marie C. Foster - All rights reserved.**

The contents of this book may not be reproduced, duplicated or transmitted without direct written permission from the author.

Under no circumstances will any legal responsibility or blame be held against the publisher for any reparation, damages, or monetary loss due to the information herein, either directly or indirectly.

Legal Notice:

This book is copyright protected. This is only for personal use. You cannot amend, distribute, sell, use, quote or paraphrase any part or the content within this book without the consent of the author.

Disclaimer Notice:

Please note the information contained within this document is for educational and entertainment purposes only. Every attempt has been made to provide accurate, up to date and reliable complete information. No warranties of any kind are expressed or implied. Readers acknowledge that the author is not engaging in the rendering of legal, financial, medical or professional advice. The content of this book has been derived from various sources. Please consult a licensed professional before attempting any techniques outlined in this book.

By reading this document, the reader agrees that under no circumstances are is the author responsible for any losses, direct or indirect, which are incurred as a result of the use of information contained within this document, including, but not limited to, —errors, omissions, or inaccuracies.

Table of Contents

Introduction

Chapter 1: Getting Started with Toddler Potty Training

Chapter 2: Potty Training Preparation

Chapter 3: Proper Communication Tips

Chapter 4: Toilet Introduction

Chapter 5: How to Apply the Two-Day Method

Chapter 6: How to Apply a Diaper-Free Solution

Chapter 7: Potty Training:

Mistakes to Avoid

Chapter 8: Potty Training – Tips for Boys

Chapter 9: Potty Training – Tips for Girls

BONUS Chapter: Helpful Tips for Dads

Conclusion

Introduction:

The first year of your baby's life is incredible, as you marvel in all the developmental milestones that they achieve. It is beautiful watching your little one as they learn to pick up their head, then crawl, and start to explore the world around them. Something you must consider as they age, however, is the right time to start potty training.

Toilet training can be separated into two separate approaches. The first is the 'wait-for-your-toddler-to-be-ready' approach, which is generally a lot longer than early potty training. The second is teaching your kid when you believe they are developmentally ready. There are numerous advantages to this, including an easier and quicker training process (because your child has not yet developed bad habits like stubbornness or getting used to the feeling of pee or poop in their diaper), a higher level of self-esteem and independence for your child, and less money spent on diapers over your child's lifetime.

Once you realize that the best method is to get your child ready for potty training, instead of waiting for them to be ready, the next step is to read through the pages of this book. If you are a busy parent, this 2-day method is ideal. You can choose to potty train your toddler in a single weekend, rather than needing to find the time to stretch it over three days, as is common with the 3-day method.

In this book, you are going to learn how to prepare yourself (and your little one) for toddler potty training. You will learn what to buy beforehand, the best methods of convincing your son or daughter to climb onto the potty, and how to reward them, to make sure that using the toilet becomes a habit.

For parents who have spoken to others about potty training, heard horror stories or developed struggles of their own, skepticism might be at the front of their minds when they hear that the toddler potty training method only takes two days. However, as a parent who has tried this method out personally, I can say that it really does work. The two-day method was effective and while it did require a great deal of commitment the weekend that I put it into practice, it was well worth it. By the end of the weekend, my toddler was a potty trained champ!

Truthfully, even if you are skeptical, there is almost nothing to lose from trying this method. You will purchase the things that you would have to purchase when your child was ready anyway, like underwear and a potty chair. Aside from these costs, the only thing that you must commit to the process is your time. Since it is designed to fit into a single weekend, this is hardly a sacrifice.

So, what do you have to lose? Prepare yourselves and gear up for the next weekend you have free and make it all about getting your little one to put their pee and poop where it belongs. It is a small time commitment that is well worth it.

Best of luck on your potty training journey!

Chapter 1: Getting Started with Toddler Potty Training

Chapter 1: Getting Started with Toddler Potty Training

Children become toddlers when they reach certain developmental milestones between 1 and 2 years of age. It is during this time when they may start moving around more, try (and eventually succeed) at walking, and start expanding their vocabulary. The toddler stage is also characterized by an increased awareness of the child's surroundings, a desire for great independence, recognition of the toddler's own person and that of others, imitation of behavior and even defiant behavior. While this milestone means many things, it can also indicate that your child is ready to start toddler potty training.

What is Toddler Potty Training?

Toddler potty training does not really relate to a specific age of potty training. Typically, it takes place before the child indicates being ready, which is common when parents take the more relaxed approach to toilet training. Toddler potty training describes any toilet training that is initiated by the parent, though it usually takes place between 1 and 2 years of age.

When Should I Start Toddler Potty Training?

It is entirely up to you when you start potty training. You should note, however, that your child should be able to do several things before you start the process. Before starting, make sure that your toddler can:

- Walk to the toilet or potty training chair
- Say at least a few words, indicating that they can communicate with you when they have to go to the toilet
- Show that he/she wants to please you, or at least has a potty-training receptive attitude

If your child has reached these developmental milestones, then your little one may be ready for potty training.

The 3-Day Method of Toilet Training vs. the 2-Day Methods

One of the most popular methods of potty training is the 3-day method, which gives your toddler an extra day to work on getting the potty technique down to a fine art. Unfortunately, not all parents can work with the 3-day method, especially those who work during the week or who have busy lifestyles. While many of the techniques used are similar, doing the work in 2 days lets you schedule it in for the weekend.

Why Toilet Training Your Toddler is Important

Some parents and experts recommend that you allow your child to start potty training when ready. You should familiarize them with the toilet and praise them if they want to use it, but generally, allow the toddler to decide when they are ready themselves.

The problem with the 'wait-until-your-child-is-ready' method of potty training is that it can take significantly longer to convince your child to start using the toilet. This is okay for some families, but it does restrict what your child can do. For example, most preschools and some daycares require that a child is potty trained before attending. This lets the teachers and caregivers give all the children the attention and time that is needed for learning, rather than spending their time worrying about which child needs to use the bathroom.

Benefits of Early Toilet Training

In some cultures and the western world specifically, it has become a popular trend to let children decide when they are ready to potty train, rather than encouraging them early on. Early toilet training does not include training as an infant, but takes place between the ages of 1 and 2, once the child meets the right developmental milestones. This is considered early because the waiting method usually takes place after 2 ½ years of age. Some of the benefits of encouraging your child to potty train sooner include:

- Less Time to Form Bad Habits- As your toddler becomes more self-aware, the child will start to recognize the sensations of peeing and pooping inside their diaper. This familiarity becomes detrimental the longer that you wait to potty train them because they will become comfortable having the waste inside their pants. This habit can be hard to break, especially when they are more interested in things like eating, watching television or playing rather than taking the few minutes break needed to use the restroom.

- Less Defiance- The younger a child is, the more likely it is that they will respond well to their parents' encouragement during toilet training. After two, toddlers tend to become more defiant and less likely to care about pleasing, as they start to challenge their parents' authority and push boundaries. This newfound defiance does not stop as they age, so teaching your toddler

before he or she enters this stage can greatly increase the likelihood of success.
- Better Awareness of Bowel Signals- Not only does peeing and pooping in a diaper become a habit as your toddler ages, so does ignoring the signals that the body sends when it needs to eliminate waste. This makes it less likely that your child will pay attention enough to the signals to stop what they are doing at the time and use the toilet.

In addition to avoiding some of the unpleasant effects of waiting too long to potty train your toddler, here are some advantages:

- Lowers the Cost of Parenting- When you train your child to use the bathroom earlier, you ultimately spend less money on diapers and pull-ups. The method described in this book does not recommend the use of pull-ups at all, so it will drastically reduce the amount you spend on diapers throughout your child's life.

- Lowers Impact on the Environment- Did you know that the average disposable diaper can lie around for 500 years before decomposing? Not only are you saving money by purchasing fewer diapers, you are contributing to the environment in a positive way.
- Improves Self-Esteem and Independence- As your child matures, they will take pleasure in their milestones and

development. This is especially true as you praise them. By teaching your child to potty train earlier, you can increase their sense of capability and independence. This, in turn, increases their self-esteem and confidence.

- Benefits Your Child's Health and Hygiene- With potty training should come positive hygiene habits like hand washing. This encourages good health. Additionally, you have to worry less about irritation and diaper rash once your child is no longer sitting in wet diapers for a long period of time.
- More Flexibility for Daycare and School- If your child is not toilet trained, you may find that certain

daycares and schools will not accept them as a student. If your child already has good bathroom habits, you will not have to stress about how long they are sitting in their diaper at the daycare or if they will be accepted to preschool.

Overview of the 2-Day Potty Training Method

As you read this book, we will go over how to train your 2-year old in detail. Before we get started, here are the basic steps you can expect.

1. Preparing Your Child for Potty Training- Before you get started, you will need a specific strategy to teach your child to use the toilet.

2. Teaching Toilet Communication- If your child cannot tell you that they need to pee or poop, it will be very hard for them to start potty training.

3. Introducing Your Child to the Toilet- Before your child will willingly sit on the potty, you must teach them about the toilet and what it is for.

4. Applying the 2-Day Method of Potty Training- This will go over potty training boot camp, where your child will learn all the skills they need to stay dry during the day.

In addition to details about the 2-day potty training process above, you will learn the best way to get your child to stay diaper free, common mistakes that you should avoid for toilet training success and bonus tips for girls, boys and dads.

CHAPTER SUMMARY:

1. Toddler potty training describes any early training initiated by the parent, rather than waiting for cues from the child that he or she is ready. Usually, this occurs between the first and second years of a child's life, when the toddler can communicate, is able to walk to the toilet, and has a willing attitude toward doing what their caregiver requests. That is when the 2-day method will be most effective.

2. There are many benefits for the 2-day method when compared against the wait-for-the-toddler method. Toddlers are often more eager to please during

this time and have not yet developed 'bad' potty habits, like ignoring their bodily signals that they have to pee or poop or sitting in a dirty diaper. Additionally, you save money on diapers and lessen your impact on the environment.

3. The 2-day potty training technique is ideal for parents who have a busy schedule and need to fit the training into a 2-day weekend. By committing your time, you will easily be able to use the procedure described in this book to convince your toddler to use the toilet.

YOUR QUICK START ACTION STEP: FIND MORE INFORMATION

If you do not want to skim the pages of this book, or you have a question that has not been answered yet, find out a little more about the 2-day method of potty training by reading at least one website. You can also compare methods if you would like to, to see which technique is best for you and your child.

Chapter 2: Potty Training Preparation

Chapter 2: Potty Training Preparation

Potty training is not something that will happen without work. You cannot 'wing it' or just do it. Rather, toilet training is something that you must plan for. You will need to buy a few things to set your child up for success and have a well-thought-out, strategic plan of action to get potty training done over the weekend.

Why You Need a Strategic Plan for Potty Training

Let me tell you why 'just doing it' is a mistake. My son was around 15 months old when he showed an interest in the potty for the first time. As a new parent,

I was excited. I could hardly believe that it would be that simple. I jumped into it with both feet, giving him plenty of praise each time that he went on the potty and asking him several times a day if he needed to go.

While I thought this would be enough, we lacked a lot of consistency. The times that I did catch him were flukes and, months later, he was still not fully trained. Some days, he would not go on the toilet at all because we were busy and he still did not understand how to ask to use the potty.

Had I taken the time to do a little more research, I probably would have had a much easier time potty training. I was fortunate enough with my daughter that I had already done the research for her brother. When she showed interest around 17 months, we tried the 2-day method and it went off without a hitch. In a single weekend, she had learned what it took almost a year for our son to learn.

Benefits of Developing a Strategic Potty Training Plan

Strategic planning comes with many benefits that make it ideal in any situation, not just while toilet training. Even so, here are some ways that coming up with a clear potty training plan can help get your child on track:

- Clear End Goal- When you plan, you can see the end goal very clearly. Following this 2-day crash course, the ideal situation is that your child becomes familiar enough with the toilet that they choose not to go to the bathroom in their underpants. Ideally, you should be able to leave them in underwear and not worry too much about accidents. They may happen from time to time, but the goal of potty training is to minimize them.

- Establishing Direction- Once you know where the end goal is, you can establish the direction that you want potty training to take. This includes the way that you introduce and describe the toilet to your toddler. Make sure as you do this that you are clear about your expectations that you expect them to go pee and poop in the toilet from now on.

- Offering Consistent Rewards- One of the biggest problems I had when training my first son was inconsistency, both with rewards and going to the bathroom. When you develop a strategic plan and put it into action, the rewards (and the message you are trying to send your toddler) is consistent.
- Clearing the Weekend- Once you have a plan, you can choose a timeframe to do it in. Stock up on snacks, juice and anything else you need to get through the weekend and keep your toddler at home. You can have visitors over, but be sure to stick to the potty training schedule regardless of who is around. Consistently paying attention to your little

one's 'potty' signals and regularly getting them on the toilet is critical if you want to have success with the 2-day method.

- Giving Your Toddler Goals- One of the great things that comes along with potty training is boosted self-esteem and independence. If you come up with a goal and share it with your toddler, they are going to revel in their accomplishments, too. They are going to know exactly what you expect them to do and when they find themselves capable of it, they will have a newfound confidence and gratification in potty training.

How to Develop a Toddler Potty Training Strategy

Now, you know that planning is critical to toilet training success, it's time to go over the steps that will get you there. Coming up with a strategy is not just jotting down a few ideas on a piece of paper and calling it done. Follow this process for success with your strategic planning.

1. Do Your Research- If you followed the quick-action plan suggested at the end of the first chapter, you might have already had a jumpstart on this. The first thing that you should do is check out a few different potty training strategies. For parents who are worried about their child going potty on the carpet, consider choosing a warm day and letting your little one run around

naked in the backyard. As you choose the methods that you implement, however, keep in mind your toddler's personality and what will be most effective for him or her and least stressful for you. Doing this gives you the greatest chance of toilet training success.

2. Decide What Plan to Implement- After plenty of research, you will have a clear picture of the many techniques that can be used for potty training. Once you have decided, move onto the next steps of planning.

3. The Great Underwear Debate- One of the biggest horrors of toilet training is the realization that your little one's pee and poop is not going to be contained by a diaper. Pull-ups can work for some children, but they are less likely to work

because they are so close to being a diaper. Even the ones with the cool-touch that happens when your child pees or poops may not cause them to understand the relations between the bladder and bowel movement and understand how it feels when they have to go. For this reason, many people recommend moving straight to underwear with potty training. If you do choose this, make sure to stack up on plenty of undies before the big weekend.

4. Stock Up on Rewards- Before you get started, you will have to decide how you want to reward your little one for their efforts. Choose a small candy (like chocolate chips), stickers, or something else your toddler is interested in. You should also prepare yourself to be available for plenty of praise to go with

whatever treat that you choose as a reward. It can also be helpful to differentiate between pees and poops by offering a second small candy or a large sticker rather than a small one for when your toddler does number two. Put off visits to the park and grandma's house and go shopping before you start the potty training journey. This way, there will be no distractions from toilet training.

6. Communicate with Your Toddler- It is best to potty train after you have had at least a few days to get your child excited about the weekend to come. Always explain the upcoming toilet training crash course as something exciting that you are going to do together. You could also take him/her to the bathroom with you, their other parent, or an older

sibling, so they can see how their role models use their toilet.

7. Get it done- Once you have considered all these areas, its time to write out the plan. Decide what you need to buy and prepare your toddler for the upcoming weekend, by showing plenty of excitement.

CHAPTER SUMMARY:

1. Developing a strategic plan for potty training is critical to toilet training success. If you try to implement toilet training without a plan, you may lack the consistency that is necessary to make your little one start using the toilet. Having a plan lets you prepare better, develop consistency and focus on

the end goal, all of which are going to improve your efforts.

2. When you fail to plan, you plan to fail. By coming up with a strategy that will work for you and your toddler, you ultimately set yourselves up for potty training success. Additionally, you gain the benefits of knowing exactly what to do over the upcoming weekend and are able to prepare, so you do not have to leave the house during boot camp.

3. You can come up with a descriptive toilet training strategy in 7 simple steps. Remember to consider your child's personality as you develop the strategy for optimal success. Then, decide on factors like whether you will use underwear or pull-ups (or let them wear nothing at all), when the potty training will take place, and how your child will

communicate and be rewarded each time that they need to go.

YOUR QUICK START ACTION STEP: KEEP LEARNING

Spend several minutes checking out different potty training techniques as was suggested in Step 1. This will prepare you to come up with a strategic plan that works, rather than choosing one and hoping for the best. Once you have done this and decided what method to use, turn the page to the next chapter and start the next step of the 2-day potty training journey.

Chapter 3: Proper Communication Tips

Chapter 3: Proper Communication Tips

Picture this. It is 1950s America and disposable diapers have yet to hit the shelves. Each time that your little one decides to soil his or her cloth diaper, you must rinse or scrub the diaper, as well as your toddler's bottom. This is a tiring and tedious process, one that you would like to do as little as possible.

The only logical solution during these earlier days was to potty train—early. Each time that the baby went in the toilet represented another cloth diaper that didn't need to be rinsed and washed. These small victories would lead to potty training much earlier than is the standard now—by the age of 2.

One of the reasons credited by doctors is because children are not emotionally ready for toilet training until they are between 2 and 3. The fast-paced lifestyle that many parents lead may also be to blame, as time being a parent, working, and attending to the many commitments that come along with having children take up time. Even so, it is not uncommon for younger children to be toilet trained—it is common practice for children in Eastern Europe, Asia, Latin America and Africa to have their children toilet trained by 2 years of age.

This proves that it is possible to communicate with your child, even when they are in the earlier years of their life. This chapter will teach you about why this communication is important and how you can develop potty training communication between yourself and your toddler. This will lead to toilet training success.

What is Successful Toilet Training Communication?

Successful potty training communication describes a communication relationship that goes both ways. You must communicate what you want your toddler to do in a way that they understand and are willing. However, you must also be receptive to the communication signals that your toddler is sending out to you.

When I was potty training my youngest, we spent plenty of time on doing research before the big weekend. We wanted to take the proper steps, so we didn't develop the same problems with her that we had with our son. One thing that we paid close attention to leading up to the big day was her pottying habits. Even though she didn't know the words yet, our daughter was letting us know with her body movements when she needed to go. It almost seemed like she was embarrassed about pooping because she would go into a corner or hide under a table before doing her business. She also still got the 'shivers' that babies sometimes get following a pee. Once we recognized the signals that she was sending us, we could teach her the words for pee and poop.

I think the communication between myself and our daughter was a big help in the process. She learned to identify them as 'ee' and 'oo' (she couldn't pronounce a 'P' sound yet) and we responded by getting her to the potty as quickly as possible. After a few rounds of this, she started to head toward the toilet herself, shrieking 'ee' or 'oo' on her way.

We were fortunate enough to recognize our daughter's signals early on, which gave us a jumpstart on communication. Even if you aren't sure where to start, this chapter is going to teach you what you need to know. By the end, you will have the steps necessary to create a positive result connecting and communicating with your toddler as you potty train.

Why Communication is Important

Have you ever heard a word you were unfamiliar with? You probably never came across it before, nor have you heard it said by someone else. In this situation, you either asked what the other person meant or used context clues to figure out what was going on.

Your child's brain is much less-developed than that of an adult. As your toddler learns and grows, they form connections in the brain that relate certain sensations and feelings to the words that you give them. When you begin potty training, it is unlikely that your child associates the feeling of peeing or pooping as the sensation of needing to eliminate waste. It becomes your job to develop this communication.

Don't worry if you are unsure of how to do that—we will go over the steps you need to take in the next section.

Benefits of Establishing a Communication Connection during Toilet Training

- Your Toddler Can Tell You When They Need to Go- Even though the 2-day method requires you to spend every moment of the day with your child, you may miss a cue. They may sneak away to the corner to use the bathroom at first, or they simply might lack the mental connection that indicates the sensation they are feeling is needing to pee or poop. Once you teach them the words and connect them with the sensations they are experiencing by using elimination communication, however, most of the hard part of potty training is over.

- You Can Clearly Communicate Your Pride- Using the toilet is a huge deal for your toddler. When you toilet train earlier, you have the advantage of still working with a toddler who is receptive to making you happy. Rather than being defiant and resistant, the communication you develop will encourage them to share in the happiness with you and do what you want them to.
- You Can Encourage Your Child to Share and Ask Questions- While going to the bathroom is simple for adults, it can seem intimidating to a toddler. When

you have open communication, your toddler feels comfortable asking questions and sharing the way that their body is feeling. This increases the chance of success.

- You Build Your Relationship with Your Toddler- Your child is going to look to you for guidance during this major milestone in their life. This is especially true for older children, who have started to use the bathroom in their diapers and felt the sensations already. As you accomplish potty training together, the connection and communication between you and your toddler will strengthen your relationship.

How to Connect with Your Child for Potty Training

Elimination communication is critical to potty training success, especially for younger children who are still identifying their bodily sensations and how they relate to eliminating waste. To form a solid communication connection that will form the foundation for toilet training, use the following steps.

1. Educate Your Child through Observation- One of the easiest ways to start teaching your child about the potty is to take them along with you when you use the toilet. Make grunting noises while you are pooping and after you finish, let them see it in the bowl. Toddlers tend to follow their parents to the bathroom anyway, so don't resist next time. Be sure to communicate what

you are doing, using phrases like pee, poop, and 'going potty.' Also, don't forget to wash your hands afterward!

2. Rely on the Power of Media- Toddlers are very visual learners, because one of the things that they can easily relate to their senses is what they are seeing. For this reason, movies, books and television shows are all useful tools when it comes to toilet training your little one. They can often explain areas where parents are unclear or confusing to their little one. If your child doesn't seem to be as interested in the basic potty training media, consider finding shows with their favorite characters to teach them how to go. Some well-known books and movies are by Sesame Street, Dora, Daniel Tiger and Caillou. Others involve princesses, superheroes, or just the average girl or

boy. If you fancy a project, work together with your child to describe the process and create your own potty training book. Another great choice are baby dolls that 'pee' or 'poop' in their pants. Use them to teach your child about where pee and poop comes out and where they need to go when they eliminate waste.

3. Watch for Specific Indicators- For each child, there is usually a telltale sign that indicates they need to use the bathroom. This could include moving around, holding their private areas, hiding in a corner or making a specific sound. By paying attention to these indicators, you can help your toddler understand the relationship between the way they are feeling and needing to go on the toilet for elimination.

4. Encourage Your Child to Communicate Their Ideas and Experience- About a year after our oldest was potty trained, he became obsessed with tacking the word 'poop' onto everything. He could be saying worse things, but it bothered me that he had developed such a 'potty' mouth. While your child is learning to use the toilet, however, there is nothing wrong with this type of talk. Encourage your child to talk about their experience and share thoughts about the way they are feeling when they need to use the bathroom. Being encouraging and receptive to whatever they say about the toilet training process will open the channels of communication and encourage them to share more. This is critical for potty training success.

5. Keep Potty Training Talk Positive- One of the biggest mistakes that parents make when potty training is making it seem as if having an accident is a big deal. The 2-day method can become frustrating, especially if you choose to go with the generally more effective 'no underwear' route. Do not make a big deal about messes—just clean them up. Then, when you can, put the mess into the toilet and explain to your child that he or she should make those types of messes in the potty from now on. Making your toddler feel ashamed about accidents is not just discouraging—it can create negative associations with the toilet training process and cause them to take longer to potty train.

6. Make Sure They Know You Are Proud- As you are minimizing accidents,

you should also be praising your toddler each time that they are successful on the potty. Offer plenty of praise and affection and make sure they know that you are proud of their accomplishments on the toilet. This positive reinforcement will make your toddler feel good about what they are doing on the potty and you will feel good about it, too.

CHAPTER SUMMARY:

1. Successful elimination communication means simply that there is an open channel of communication between yourself and your toddler. He or she should become more comfortable communicating their emotions about potty training, as well as when they need to go. You also must communicate your

expectations with your toddler in a positive way, both as you are preparing and during the potty training process. Another part of good communication is being receptive, by responding to your toddler's questions and ensuring they are responsive to the positive feedback you are giving them when they go on the toilet.

2. There are many benefits of establishing open channels of communication between yourself and your child in all areas of parenting. When used for potty training, elimination communication helps clarify times when your child needs to pee or poop, makes your child feel your confidence and pride, encourages your toddler to share and ask questions, and improves your relationship overall.

3. There are several steps that go into developing positive potty training communication between yourself and your child. These include providing the right tools and materials for observation and helping your child learn what to do, watching for indicators that your toddler needs to use the toilet, providing plenty of positive communication and downplaying accidents. By doing these things, you will foster good communication and make the potty training process significantly easier on both of you.

YOUR QUICK START ACTION STEP: START COMMUNICATING ABOUT POTTY TRAINING

It is never too early to start familiarizing your toddler with what happens on the potty. Encourage them to share bathroom time with you and learn about peeing and pooping, through observation and the many media options available. It is also a good time to introduce materials like potty training books and movies. These things and plenty of talking about the weekend that is coming up are essential to getting your communication channels open and preparing for the upcoming lessons.

Chapter 4: Toilet Introduction

Chapter 4: Toilet Introduction

This chapter is going to be the first action step in introducing your child to the toilet. While some ideas were provided in the previous chapter, this will go more into depth about how you should introduce your toddler to the toilet.

Understanding the Toilet: What Your Toddler Needs to Know

How you introduce the toilet to your child is critical to potty training failure or success. There are several areas that you should address, including:

- Where Waste Goes- The major goal of potty training is teaching your toddler where pee and poop are supposed to go. Some parents have fun teaching their child that the toilet is 'eating' their waste, but this can be scary to some. Use your best judgment to decide what will work best with your toddler.
- Who Goes on the Potty- When you are amping up your child for going to the restroom, it may be a good idea to show them television shows or books where their favorite characters eliminate waste in the toilet. You could also praise older children (like an older sibling or cousin) who uses the big potty and how proud their parents must be. By giving your

child role models that they want to be like and relating this to going to the toilet, your child will want to eliminate waste on the toilet as well.

- Wiping- While getting your toddler to go in the toilet is the major milestone that you are trying to meet, familiarizing them with wiping at this stage can be very helpful later, once they have mastered using the potty.
- Bathroom Hygiene- In addition to the basics of using the toilet, you should teach your child bathroom hygiene. Be sure to emphasize washing hands each time that your toddler uses the potty, especially if he or she enjoys washing their hands.

Benefits of the Pre-Game Warm up

One of the reasons that we were skeptical about the 2-day method with our daughter was because it did not seem possible that she could learn in such a short time. It is more practical, however, to think of the two days that you are heavily focusing on toilet training as a sort of boot camp and remember that the pre-game warm up is important as the actual game. It helps prep your toddler, so when the big weekend does come, they are more than ready to show you what they can do. Here are some of the benefits of preparing your child well before the weekend:

- It Starts Shaping Your Child's Expectations- When you are

collaborating with someone else, one of the most common reasons for disappointment is unclear expectation. When you consistently relate peeing and pooping to the bathroom and provide positive feedback when he or she shows an interest, they become familiar with the potty training process and what is expected of them.

- You Have Time to Promote the Idea- The 2-day method is incredibly effective for children who are ready—but you must ensure your toddler is ready before the weekend happens for it to be a success. By introducing the idea before your toddler is put to the test, you give them time to get familiar with the idea.

- You Can Let Your Child Pick Their Tools- Letting your child choose their potty chair or picking out underwear with their favorite character on them can be incredibly beneficial as an incentive to get the job done. It may provide just the motivation that they need to propel them toward success. Additionally, by letting your child pick out new undies and a potty chair to use, it helps build the excitement for the weekend to come.
- It Lets You Determine if Your Child is Really Ready- There are some people who will tell you that regardless of what you do, you cannot force a child who is not ready. However, the people who say that are often working with

older children who have started to show their individuality and defiance. They may fight against each of their parents' attempts at training them because they have already become accustomed to doing whatever they want and just using their diaper when they have to go. When you are dealing with a younger child, as you often are when using this earlier method of potty training, it is more likely that it will be effective. Additionally, by pre-gaming and exploring the idea of potty training before the big weekend, you can use your own judgment as to if your little one is ready to start using the toilet.

Steps for Effective Toilet Introduction

As you get started, be sure to keep the following steps in mind:

1. Let Them Accompany You to the Bathroom- If you listen to any parent, they may tell you that trying to go to the bathroom alone is a nightmare. When you are considering potty training, however, use this to your advantage. Show your little one how to go on the potty by making encouraging noises and explaining what you are doing. You can also let them observe older siblings, when appropriate.

2. Decide on a Method of Education- As mentioned earlier, there are several ways to educate your child about toilet training. You can find books or movies

dedicated to potty training or use a 'potty' baby doll. By education your little one, you will answer questions that they may not know how to ask yet. Remember that curiosity is a good thing. It shows that using the bathroom has piqued your child's interest.

3. Buying Their Own Potty- As you choose a toilet, you have the option of picking one that sits on the ground or one that sits on top of the toilet seat in your bathroom, along with a stool so your toddler can get up to the toilet. The one that sits on top of the toilet can be a good option if it seems he or she is interested in using the toilet where you go. The ones that sit on the floor, however, have the advantage of being portable so you can set them in whatever room your child is in and quickly get

them to the potty. You can also choose to invest in both.

4. Choosing Underwear- 'Big girl' or 'big boy' underwear are a great incentive for children learning to potty train. If you do decide that you do not want to use the 'no underpants' method, then you should have your child choose two types of underwear—some plain undies with a little extra padding for the weekend of training and some character underwear to use as a reward once your toddler has been successful at potty training.

CHAPTER SUMMARY:

1. There are several things that you should familiarize your little one with before beginning their potty training journey. This includes demonstrating

how to use the potty, educating them with media and other materials, introducing wiping, and encouraging good bathroom hygiene.

2. When you take the time to warm-up your toddler to the idea of toilet training before their big weekend, you make it more likely that they will have success. The benefits of doing this include establishing expectations, giving your child time to think about the idea and ask questions, allowing them to pick their underwear and toilet, and helping you decide if you and your toddler are ready for potty training boot camp.

3. The steps provided in this chapter will help make introducing the toilet easier. This is a critical step before moving onto potty training boot camp. The best way to do this is through demonstration,

them to the potty. You can also choose to invest in both.

4. Choosing Underwear- 'Big girl' or 'big boy' underwear are a great incentive for children learning to potty train. If you do decide that you do not want to use the 'no underpants' method, then you should have your child choose two types of underwear—some plain undies with a little extra padding for the weekend of training and some character underwear to use as a reward once your toddler has been successful at potty training.

CHAPTER SUMMARY:

1. There are several things that you should familiarize your little one with before beginning their potty training journey. This includes demonstrating

how to use the potty, educating them with media and other materials, introducing wiping, and encouraging good bathroom hygiene.

2. When you take the time to warm-up your toddler to the idea of toilet training before their big weekend, you make it more likely that they will have success. The benefits of doing this include establishing expectations, giving your child time to think about the idea and ask questions, allowing them to pick their underwear and toilet, and helping you decide if you and your toddler are ready for potty training boot camp.

3. The steps provided in this chapter will help make introducing the toilet easier. This is a critical step before moving onto potty training boot camp. The best way to do this is through demonstration,

sharing of the ideas of potty training, and choosing a toilet and 'big' kid underwear.

YOUR QUICK START ACTION STEP: SCHEDULE POTTY TRAINING LEARNING TIMES

Get out your calendar now and write down the date that you should have your child familiarized with the toilet. Ideally, you should finish doing this the week prior to potty training boot camp. This is far enough from the date to get them excited, but close enough that they will stay excited as they anticipate the important weekend to come.

Chapter 5: How to Apply the Two-Day Method

Chapter 5: How to Apply the Two-Day Method

After reading the previous chapters, you should be almost ready to get started on the 2-day method of toilet training. This will go over the plan in depth, so you know exactly what to expect over the weekend.

Why the 2-Day Method Works

The basic principles behind the 2-day method are similar to the more popular 3-day method. However, for parents that work during the week, it is a lot more convenient and easier to apply than a method that takes three days.

The 2-day method works because you spend plenty of time getting your child familiar with the toilet and what is expected of him or her. Once you have done this, your toddler is mentally prepared to take the next step.

One of the key components of a successful 2-day boot camp for potty training is having a child who is willing to please their parents. This is the reason that it is typically recommended that younger children (between 1 and 2) are trained using this method. You may have success for other ages, but it may be more difficult because the child has already developed their own attitude. They also have learned to ignore their bodily urges or go in their diaper because it is convenient.

Finally, you will notice that the 2-day method emphasizes letting your little one run around without underpants on. This is the best technique because it teaches them the sensations associated with peeing and pooping. The speed that it works at makes it convenient since you can do it over the weekend or on a short family vacation.

Benefits of the 2-Day Method

As mentioned before, following the steps provided are essential to potty training success. There are numerous benefits that come along with this method. Here is a brief reminder:

- It is a no-hassle way to potty train since toddlers quickly learn what is expected of them.

- You can move straight from diapers to underwear, eliminating the need for expensive pull-ups.
- By training at a younger age, you lessen your impact on the environment because of disposable diapers, without having to scrub cloth diapers for the next couple years of your child's life.
- Children are generally less defiant and more eager to please, so they will be easier to communicate with about the potty.
- The 2-day method also quickly boosts your child's self-esteem, confidence, and independence, because it sets them up for success (and plenty of praise from you).

- It is a quick method of training that can be done in a single weekend, which is great for busy families.

How to Potty Train in 2 Days

Now that you have all the background knowledge needed, here is the most effective way to train your toddler to use the potty in just two days:

Step 1: Say Bye to the Diaper

Day One of potty training boot camp starts off as your child gets out of bed. Hand him or her a drink to start the day and walk them to the garbage can. Have them remove their diaper, put it in the can, and say goodbye. Do not give them the option of wearing a diaper for the rest of the weekend.

Step 2: Give an Explanation

Shortly after, explain to your toddler why you are not putting a diaper on them. You can let them run around naked or put them in a long nighty or t-shirt. Just be sure to keep their bottom exposed. Then, lead them over to the toilet and encourage them to try it out. Explain that they will not have a diaper to catch their mess for the day, so the potty is where it needs to go.

Step 3: Have Breakfast

Next, sit down for breakfast. Let your child have another drink. Shortly after you have finished eating (or sooner if they indicate they need to go), take your toddler to the potty. This is likely to be a successful trip since it has followed two drinks and a meal.

Step 4: Stop at Regular Intervals for Reminders

The next two days, you will stay in the house and follow this routine. The best thing to do is take your child every 15 minutes, especially if you are trying to avoid an accident. Each time that he or she is successful do not forget to give plenty of praise and affection, along with the reward that you have chosen for your child.

Step 5: Slow Down on Drinks about an Hour before Sleep

As it approaches your toddler's naptime, cut off the drinks. Make sure to put him or her to bed after a successful toilet attempt. Some will recommend training for the day and night at different times, but it is least confusing if you do not put a diaper back on your child for the entire potty training boot camp. You will want to repeat this ceasing of liquids and foods about an hour before bed at night. Make sure your little one uses the bathroom before going to bed and put down a plastic mattress cover if you are overly concerned about accidents.

Step 6: Wake Your Little One at Night

About half way through the night, you will want to set the alarm to wake your toddler up to go potty. This is a trip that you and he/she will not enjoy, but it is necessary to help train their body to wake up and potty, rather than just going in a diaper and staying in the wetness all night.

Step 7: Do it Again the Next Day

Follow the same ritual on the second day, encouraging your little one to go often and pushing the drinks. You will be surprised how quickly they catch on. Once Monday rolls around, they will be more than ready to don their 'big' kid underwear and handle the day.

Bonus Step: Remember to Stay Positive

Expect your child to have accidents, even if you walk him or her to the toilet every 15 minutes. When it happens, calmly clean the mess and explain where he/she should be eliminating waste. Keep your attitude calm and positive. When they do pee or poop, remember what a big deal it is to them (and you). Celebrate each of their successes and in no time, you will have a positively potty trained toddler.

CHAPTER SUMMARY:

1. The 2-day method is most effective on toddlers who are eager to please their parents and who have not yet developed the habit of sitting in a soiled diaper. By preparing your child and introducing them to the toilet before the actual boot camp, you set them up for success.

2. Remember that your child's success will come with many benefits. It can be tough to fit a whole weekend in where you just stay at home with your toddler, but it is well worth it as you boost your child's independence and lower your cost of diapers and impact on the environment.

3. By following the steps provided in this chapter, you ultimately set your toddler

up for potty training success. Offer plenty of drinks and make your little one say goodbye to their diaper—even for nap time and bedtime. Take them to the bathroom regularly, even in the middle of the night, and don't forget to react positively each time that they go to the bathroom where they are supposed to.

YOUR QUICK START ACTION STEP: SCHEDULE A WEEKEND TO GET IT DONE

Now that you have all the information you need for success, it is time to get the job done. Schedule a weekend you can stay home with your toddler and follow the steps outlined in this chapter. If you want a little extra help, read the next couple chapters for extra advice before you get started.

Chapter 6: How to Apply a Diaper-Free Solution

Chapter 6: How to Apply a Diaper-Free Solution

In this chapter, we will go over how to get your potty trained toddler out of a diaper for good. You will also learn what this means and the major benefits that your toddler gets when switching from diapers or pull-ups to underwear.

What Does Diaper-Free Mean?

Diaper-free means that you will never have to spend money on a pack of diapers or pull-ups again. You should feel confident enough in your toddler's abilities (and they should feel confident in their own abilities) that they can wear underwear all the time.

The expectation of being diaper-free is that your child will go to the bathroom in the toilet regularly. Note that this does not mean he or she will not have any accidents. Even toddlers who have been potty trained for a year or more can have the occasional mess in their pants. Here are some examples of diaper-free kids.

Katelyn is starting her first day of preschool and she must be potty trained. After a crash course over the weekend about 2 weeks before school, she started to use the toilet regularly. Even though she has been doing well, Katelyn has two accidents on the first day of school. This is a big transition for her, however, so the teacher is understanding. By the end of the first week of school, Katelyn is making it through the day without messing in her pants. She is considered diaper-free.

Jonathan is two-years old and has impressed his parents with his potty training efforts. Though he does not wear diapers during the day, he is still frequently wetting the bed at night. His mother decides to use thickly padded underwear at night to try and contain the mess. Even though needs the extra protection at night, Jonathan is still considered diaper-free.

Benefits of Being Diaper-Free

When you start toilet training your toddler, the major goal is getting them to regularly eliminate waste in the toilet. Being diaper-free means consistently avoiding diapers. This is important because it prevents regression, or, going back to poor potty training habits. In addition to keeping your toddler on track for potty training, being diaper-free comes with several other benefits, including:

- Reassures Your Child of Your Trust and Pride- When you keep your toddler out of diapers, you are reinforcing the idea that you trust them to continue using the potty. They are also reassured of how proud you are of them, which reinforces the desire to continue using the toilet.
- Eliminates the Cost of Diapers Completely- Nighttime training pants and the occasional naptime diaper can be expensive, too. By being diaper-free, you eliminate

the cost and the associated environmental impact completely.

- Prevents Regression- If you continue to put your child in diapers after the toilet training weekend, even for just naps or nighttime, it can send mixed signals. They may be less likely to learn to go while sleeping and will not pay attention to their body signals as much. In a worst-case scenario, they may also start to use the bathroom in their pants during the day, too. Staying away from diapers altogether helps prevent this.

Teaching Your Toddler to Be Diaper-Free

If potty training boot camp went well, then you already have a great start on getting your child to be diaper-free. Here is what you need to do.

Step 1: Teach Your Child to Pull Up and Down

Potty training boot camp involved keeping your little one out of underwear and diapers, so there is a chance they do not know how to pull their underwear up and down. Teach them this as part of the potty process and monitor them for the first couple days, ensuring they are moving fast enough to get the pee or poop in the toilet. You should also avoid anything with hard closures (like buttons, snaps, overalls, and onesies) once you have toilet trained your child.

Step 2: Commit to the Toilet Training Process

Once you have taught them to pull up and down, the only thing left to do is to commit to potty training fully. Do not put them in diapers or at night, or when you leave the house. Try to plan outings around being somewhere near a potty for the first week or two, or plan to make frequent stops to let your little one use the bathroom.

Step 3: Clean Messes—Don't Contain Them

If you are striving to be completely diaper-free, then you should expect messes. Try not to get upset—otherwise, your child can quickly become discouraged and give up altogether. You also should not use diapers at all. Trying to contain the mess will just teach your toddler that it is okay to eliminate in their pants sometimes.

https://www.verywellfamily.com/potty-training-problems-not-pooping-on-the-potty-2634549

https://www.thebump.com/a/potty-training-how-to-get-started-and-making-it-work

https://www.care.com/c/stories/4920/royal-flush-potty-training-strategies-that-w/

CHAPTER SUMMARY:

1. Diaper-free training involves having a child that is diaper-free, day and night. This can take some time after potty training boot camp, but you must stay

committed to it. Otherwise, your toddler may start to have accidents.

2. When you choose not to use a diaper on your child, you reassure them of your trust and confidence in them. Additionally, you eliminate the environmental impact and the cost of diapers. Finally, going diaper-free completely helps prevent regression.

3. There are a few steps you will need to take after the 2-day toilet training session to ensure your little one remains diaper-free. You should teach him or her to pull their underwear up and down, stay consistent with toilet training, and avoid using diapers altogether.

YOUR QUICK START ACTION STEP: BRUSH UP ON TIPS FOR BEING DIAPER-FREE

Now that you have an idea of how to create a completely diaper-free life for your child visit at least one website to find tips that may help you achieve this goal.

Chapter 7: Potty Training: Mistakes to Avoid

Chapter 7: Potty Training: Mistakes to Avoid

If you are a first time parent or just one who didn't quite nail potty training the first time around, you should know that mistakes happen. It is not a judgment of your parenting skill, nor does it mean you are destined for toilet training failure. The best way to avoid these mistakes is to get educated on what they are, so you can work at avoiding them.

What Are Toilet Training Mistakes?

Potty training mistakes are usually small things that you might not think of as being a problem. However, even things that seem insignificant can set your child back.

For example, Jeff's mom decided to potty train him before starting a new school. They moved to a new house the following weekend and Jeff started to have frequent accidents. Jeff's mom wonders if her methods were ineffective. The problem with this scenario is not Jeff or his mother—it is the move. Moving to a new home is a stressful life event and Jeff may have been set back by the experience.

Another example is Kristy. Kristy did amazing at boot camp, but when her family returned to their schedule the next week, she started having accidents. This likely happened because Kristy just was not ready to pay attention to her bowel movements on her own yet. She is not receiving the same attention following the weekend, so the ideas they spent creating are not being reinforced.

Why You Need to Know These Mistakes

As with many things in life, the best offense is a good defense. By knowing what the most common mistakes are and how to look for them, you can easily set you and your child up for toilet training success.

Know that these are not the only mistakes you can make, but they are the most common. Also, feel assured that these mistakes can happen to anyone—what really matters is having the strength to overcome them. Here are some of the benefits of being familiar with potty training mistakes:

- You can quickly respond to mistakes, once you identify what is causing them.
- You can prevent setbacks by quickly responding to mistakes.
- You know what to look for, should an unexpected problem arise.
- You can troubleshoot the toilet training process, especially if you are not sure the reason your toddler is struggling.

How to Avoid Potty Training Mistakes

1. Keep Your Child Hydrated

One of the biggest reasons potty training fails is because the peeing or pooping sensation is not distinct enough for children to notice it. To ensure their signals are strong enough, make sure they drink plenty of drinks throughout the weekend. Use reduced sugar (or watered down) juice to keep them hydrated.

2. Do Not Train During Times of Stress

Things like moving, getting a new pet, or starting school can be excited and fun. However, they also are not the best time to toilet train. When a child is focusing on outside factors that cause stress, whether positive or negative, it makes it hard to concentrate on their bodily sensations and if they need to use the restroom.

3. Do Not Freak Over Accidents

Once your child moves into the world of 'big boy' or 'big girl' underwear and bathroom habits, accidents are likely to happen. You may occasionally hear stories about a child who never wet his or her pants again after toilet training, but more than likely, there will be a few messes. Remember to handle these gracefully—they are natural and you do not want your child associating negative emotions with their body elimination.

4. Don't Go Back to Diapers

Following the 2-day toilet training boot camp, you should not encourage your child to use diapers any longer. Instead, make frequent stops on long car rides, plan your grocery store trips around which have potties inside, and actively work to keep your toddler dry and out of diapers. Parents who have toddlers that struggle with nighttime dryness may choose to use diapers at night. While this is not recommended, it may be a solution if your toddler is struggling with nighttime dryness.

CHAPTER SUMMARY:

1. Mistakes can happen to any parent who is training their toddler to use the toilet. Success comes from overcoming these struggles.

2. There are numerous benefits to recognizing the struggles that your child may face as they move from potty trained to completely diaper free. By expecting the occasional issue to arise,

you can quickly respond to the mistakes and prevent regression and setbacks.

3. Identifying some of the mistakes that happen during the toilet training process can stop them from happening. Be sure to train at the right time, keep your child well-fed and hydrated, avoid using diapers completely, and remain calm and supportive in the face of accidents.

YOUR QUICK START ACTION STEP:

While this information is sufficient for prevention of problems that commonly arise, you should still educate yourself on what else may go wrong. Do not scare yourself away from potty training, but do prepare yourself by looking up the do's and don'ts of toilet training.

Chapter 8: Potty Training – Tips for Boys

Chapter 8: Potty Training – Tips for Boys

In this chapter, we will briefly focus on toilet training for boys. One of the major differences between toilet training boys and girls is that boys will need to be taught to stand and aim when they are ready. This chapter will go over what else you need to know.

Why You Need to Train Your Boy as a Boy

As you are training your child, you are teaching them a lot about their body. This makes it a good time to note that boys and girls are different. Developing 'boy' bathroom habits early will make it easier to teach him standing up later.

This will be necessary to prevent 'missing' the toilet in the future. Some other benefits include:

- No Need to Re-Learn- Some boys feel more comfortable sitting on the potty to pee, especially when they are first learning. If they do learn to stand and pee first, however, they will not have to re-learn this new method of peeing later.
- Improved Aim- When your toddler has more practice, he will be able to aim better.

Toddler Potty Training Tips for Boys

- Give Him Something to Aim at- Small cheerios or other things that will float are a good choice for getting your son to pee inside the potty. Simply instruct him to hold his private area and aim at the designated item. Alternatively, place a sticker on the bottom of his toilet training chair.

- Teach Him to Feel Comfortable Holding His Penis- While we always encourage children not to play with themselves in public, your son should feel comfortable holding himself and directing his stream where it needs to go. This is a great job for an older brother, dad, or an uncle to teach.

- Choose a Sitting Potty with a 'Lip'- Some children's toilets have a small hump or cup in the front, which is designed to catch your little one's flow if it shoots over the edge of the seat while he is toilet training.

CHAPTER SUMMARY:

1. Boys and girls are different, especially because boys will eventually need to learn to stand and pee.

2. Allowing your boy to learn in a 'boy-specific' toilet training manner will help prevent future struggles.

3. Some of the tips that you should employ while teaching your little boy to use the bathroom include giving him something to aim at, teaching him to hold his private parts, and using a potty that has a cup or lip, to catch stray urine while he is sitting to poop.

YOUR QUICK START ACTION STEP: PLAN A 'BOY' TRAINING CAMP

Use the tips provided here to help make potty training more effective for your little boy, if you are trying to train your son. These tips are something not all parents think about and will make toilet training much simpler.

Chapter 9: Potty Training – Tips for Girls

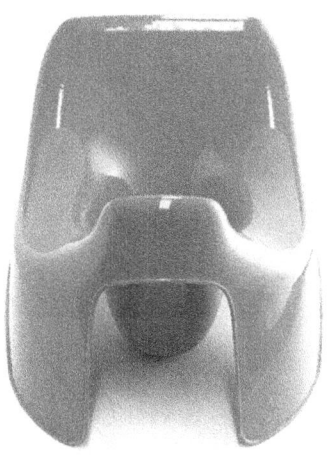

Chapter 9: Potty Training – Tips for Girls

In this chapter, we will discuss a few girl-specific tips. The major difference between girls and boys is that girls must learn how to wipe appropriately. This chapter will teach you more about this, as well as some bonus tips for training your little girl.

Why You Need to Potty Train Your Girl as a Girl

There are two major distinctions between boys and girls. The first is whether they sit or stand to pee and the second is wiping. Wiping can become a hygiene issue if it is not done properly. You must train your little girl to wipe from front to back and to clean every time that she pees. The benefits include:

- Less Chance of Infection- If your toddler is not wiping the right way, it can lead to irritation and infection in her private area. Proper wiping can prevent this.
- Better Cleanliness- Girls require more tact when it comes to cleaning after peeing than boys do. Getting them on the right track earlier means more cleanliness sooner.

Toddler Potty Training Tips for Girls

- Control Her Spray- Little girls can also have a problem with spraying over the front of the toilet. To prevent this, have your toddler sit with her knees slightly apart and back far enough that both her bottom and her private parts are over the toilet.

- Use a Potty Chair- For girls to pee, their pelvic muscles will need to relax and let the urine flow. It is easier to do this on a potty chair, where your daughter's feet can touch the floor.
- Encourage Proper Wiping from the Beginning- Teach your daughter to wipe until she feels dry. You should also teach her to wipe from front to back, which will prevent infection and irritation.

CHAPTER SUMMARY:

1. The major difference between toilet training girls vs. boys is how they sit/stand and the aftercare.

2. Recognizing this difference is critical to proper hygiene and toilet training success. It will also prevent infection caused by improper wiping.

3. By following tips like ensuring your toddler is positioned properly, teaching her to wipe properly, and using a toilet that sits close to the ground, you can improve your toddler's chance of toilet training success.

YOUR QUICK START ACTION STEP: PLAN FOR TRAINING YOUR LITTLE GIRL

If you have a little girl, implement the tips provided in this chapter into your toilet training plan. This will increase the chance of success.

BONUS Chapter: Helpful Tips for Dads

BONUS Chapter: Helpful Tips for Dads

The dads who potty train usually get less recognition than moms, because most people associate it with being a 'mom's' job. The ones that do, however, are real champs. Dads are typically portrayed as wanting to avoid messes. However, many take the mess that comes along with toilet training in stride and can have a sense of humor that mom might not. Here are some tips for dads who are taking on the responsibility of toddler potty training.

Why Dads Deserve (and Need) Potty Training Tips

Much of the material designed for potty training is geared toward moms, who are often credited for handling the messes that come along with raising a child, toilet training included. Even so, dads who take advantage of toilet training tips get the following benefits:

- A Better Idea of What to Expect- When you learn what tips can help you as a father trying to toilet train, you are giving yourself the advantage of knowing what is to come so you can prepare better.
- Unique Approach- Moms and dads are known for their different approaches to discipline, play time, snacking—really everything.

Potty training should not be excluded from this, especially if your toddler responds better to a dad's approach.

Toilet Training Tips for Dad

- Develop a Sense of Humor- Things are going to get 'messy' over your potty training weekend. It can be easy to freak out, especially if you are usually the one handling your toddler's messes. Even so, it is important to remain calm and collected in the face of messes and learn to laugh off what your child does. Potty training becomes a lot easier and more fun if you have a sense of humor to tackle it with.
- Come Up with a Code- Is there a particular animal you can get

your child interested in? Snakes work well because they look like the shape that is often left in the toilet after a poop. Even if your toddler isn't into snakes, though, come up with a cool 'victory' call that you can use each time that they poop in the potty. This is a fun dad-worthy technique.

- Stock Up on Area Rugs- If you really want to avoid cleaning up messes, buy some extra area rugs. You won't have to scrub too hard and you will not have to worry about losing your security deposit. Get the ones with rubber backing for extra security—especially if you want to let him or her sit on the furniture.

CHAPTER SUMMARY:

1. Even though people usually associate childcare, diaper changing, and potty training with moms, dads often have a unique approach that can be beneficial to their toddler.

2. When you check out potty training tips especially for dads, you find tips that match up with your personality. This can help you learn what to expect and help develop a potty training technique that fits perfectly with your toddler's learning abilities.

3. Having dad-friendly tips can make the toilet training process significantly easier. This includes using rubber-backed area rugs to prevent messes or staining, creating a victory cry, and having a sense of humor about toddler toilet training.

YOUR QUICK START ACTION STEP: COME UP WITH A PLAN

If you are a dad reading this chapter, then good luck as you tackle potty training with your toddler. Be sure to implement these tips as part of your plan if you believe they may make the process easier.

Conclusion

Thank you again for owning this book!

I hope this book was able to help you learn the best methods for potty training your toddler. Whether your toddler is a girl or boy, you should now be armed with the knowledge to make toilet training happen in just two days. From there, you will be able to encourage your child to go completely diaper-free and avoid potty training mistakes.

The next step is to come up with a plan and put it into action. With the knowledge you now have, the only thing left is to get the potty training weekend done.

Finally, if this book has given you value and helped you in any way, then I'd like to ask you for a favor. If you would be kind enough to leave a review for this book on Amazon, it'd be greatly appreciated!

Thank you and good luck!

www.ingramcontent.com/pod-product-compliance
Lightning Source LLC
Chambersburg PA
CBHW052206090526
44583CB00017BA/2141